CONTENTS

AN ALLIGATOR IN THE BATHROOM...

AND OTHER STORIES

CARTER LANGDALE

AN ALLIGATOR IN THE BATHROOM...

AND OTHER STORIES

JOHN BLAKE

Published by
John Blake Publishing Limited,
3 Bramber Court, 2 Bramber Road,
London W14 9PB, England

www.johnblakebooks.com

www.facebook.com/johnblakebooks ▪
twitter.com/jblakebooks ▪

First published in paperback in 2016

ISBN: 978-1-78606-138-6

British Library Cataloguing-in-Publication Data:
A catalogue record for this book is available from the British Library.

Design by www.envydesign.co.uk

Printed in Great Britain by CPI Group (UK) Ltd

1 3 5 7 9 10 8 6 4 2

Papers used by John Blake Publishing are natural, recyclable products
made from wood grown in sustainable forests. The manufacturing processes
conform to the environmental regulations of the country of origin.

Every attempt has been made to contact the relevant copyright-holders,
but some were unobtainable. We would be grateful if the appropriate
people could contact us.

And here's the happy bounding flea –
You cannot tell the he from she.
The sexes look alike, you see;
But she can tell, and so can he.

ROLAND YOUNG, 'The Flea'

For two very special people in my life,
Kerry and Tez.

1

LORD OF THE FLEAS

The British police will cheerfully deal with a drugged up loony waving a samurai sword, or a gang of football hooligans fighting with knives and broken bottles. They'll persuade a man to put the gun down and the Saturday-night drunks to go home, yet – in my time anyway – if they find a barking dog in front of them, they back away and call in the RSPCA to arrest it.

During my years of battling for animal welfare in Yorkshire, I had several encounters with pit bull terriers, one with a tosa inu (a huge red Japanese mastiff fighting dog) and others of breeds favoured by those persons in whom the police tend to have an interest. But that was always in town. Out in the countryside, I always thought I had a right to expect more animal sense from the local fuzz. Country boys, surely, sculpted from limestone and granite, men of the moors, hills and dales – they wouldn't bother me over a dog.

I don't know why I thought that, because my disillusionment came very early in my career, just qualified, new posting, keen as keen could be, a week into my dream job.

I was at home when the phone rang. In fact, I was in bed asleep. It was the desk sergeant at Scorswick police station, to say that several of his finest were being obstructed in the execution of their duties by a dog asserting its territorial rights. They'd been making a forced entry into a house and the animal didn't like it.

The story was that a lady had rung in, saying she was concerned about the old chap who lived opposite, alone with the aforesaid dog. This man was something of a recluse so not much was seen of him anyway, but there'd been no signs of life from the house for a few days now. So, said the sergeant, as it was all happening in a village not far from my house, would I kindly pop round to this address pronto and deal with the canine in question, thus allowing the constabulary to resolve the matter?

Yes, all right, so I rolled out of bed, put on my RSPCA official-issue weatherproofs – it was mid-January as well as two in the morning – and found my hat and van keys. Setting off on a ten- or fifteen-minute drive, my consoling thought was that I'd soon be back in bed. Carol, as yet neither inured to, nor scarred by, long experience as an RSPCA inspector's wife, was a quick learner and so hadn't bothered to wake up when I went. On autosnooze, she wouldn't even know I'd been out on a nocturnal call and so could continue to believe that our new life could only get better.

It's a tiny village where I was headed. Not on the way to anywhere, it's a no-through-road and, with nothing more than a church, a phone box and some houses lining an L-shaped street, plus a small manor to the side, it's about as quiet as a community can be. It used to be a station on the old railway line but not even the ghost-trains stop there any more.

I arrived to find two policemen and a WPC by the front door of one of the standard council semi-detacheds. This must have been the greatest assembly of law enforcers witnessed in that village since the Norman Conquest. In some of the other houses' bedrooms, the curtains were pulled aside for a better view of the unfolding *Heartbeat*-type drama.

'Where's Derek?' said the senior cop, miserably. He was a gaunt, elongated type, a nightmare for police-uniform suppliers and off-the-peg tailors everywhere, who tend to expect men of six-foot-three to weigh more than eight stone.

'He's retired,' said I brightly. 'I'm the new boy. Inspector Langdale. Carter Langdale.'

'Good man, Derek was,' continued PC Grim. 'No dog ever got the better of him. Mind you, he had the experience.'

'We're all fully trained,' I said. 'Six months' hard labour.' The grim one remained unimpressed. His nickname, I later learned, was Minnie, derived by evolution from Laugh a Minute.

The three coppers, repulsed by the proprietorial hound, had taken instead to looking through a small gap in the ancient army blankets which did for curtains in the sitting-room window of this fairly bedraggled-looking house. They had formed the suspicion that the old man, called Alf, was dead in his armchair. This meant they couldn't enter the house after all. They would have to wait for whichever doctor was on the roster that night as police surgeon.

We stood around in the freezing cold, wondering where doctors could be at this hour if they weren't in bed, waiting to be got up. The neighbour who had started the whole thing, a woman of considerable substance in a heavy overcoat, came out with cups of tea and told us that she did the old fellow's shopping for him. He would put a list and some money in a milk bottle, and she'd leave the goodies on the step.

Although the list often specified Knight's Castile soap and Omo detergent, it was believed that these items were for storage rather than use, saved against the Day of Judgement.

'And he has fifteen cats,' said the lady.

'Fifteen?' This was not a world record for a council house but it was still a fair number.

'Fifteen. I don't know why he stopped at fifteen but

he did. Wouldn't have no more. Maybe it's the Jellymeat Whiskas,' she said to me as the animal representative. I nodded, as if I knew what she was talking about. 'And the Go-Cat,' she added. 'It all comes in a van once a month. Boxes and boxes. Must cost a fortune. What with them and that dog . . .'

She tailed off and looked at us all for confirmation that she was right in her opinion that there was no room in her village for such wild behaviour.

As the sun rose and the first daylight outlined the silhouette of the little range of hills to the north-east, we saw the lights of a car turning off from the main road. Those headlamps pointed our way. Hurray! At last. Our saviour was turning up and parking on the end of the row of vehicles – two panda cars, my van, a Ferguson tractor and a couple of Series 1 Land-Rovers which, in most other parts of the world, would have been at the back of the farmyard with chickens living in them.

The good doctor – young, blonde hair, anorak with fur-trimmed hood – had a Datsun Bluebird, a vehicle much favoured at the time by the medical profession for its reliability, though scorned by the fashionable for its anagram 'durable dustbin'. Up the garden path she came, in a businesslike manner.

'Morning, everyone. Right. Are we ready?'

I could see a war going on in Minnie's mind. The policeman's natural respect for the professions was battling with the evidence of his eyes and ears. Here was a girl who looked as though she should be working Saturday mornings in Boots the Chemist, who sounded like Angela Rippon, yet who claimed to be a doctor in the ancient Ridings of Yorkshire.

'Er, we can't go in yet, Miss, er, I mean Doctor,' said Minnie. 'There's a dog.'

The doc looked baffled but took a pace or two back with the officers. It was time for Super Furry Animal Man to do his stuff. I leaned my patent grasper against the wall. This was a hollow pole with a braided wire running through double, making a noose at one end which I could pull tight at the other, very useful for keeping a dangerous beast away from one's trouser turn-ups.

As soon as my hand touched the door, the dog started barking again. The police had broken the lock in their earlier assault so I just kept going, and when I saw my quarry I knew I'd have no trouble. No need for the grasper. This was a fat, short-haired, brown and white Jack Russell with bulging eyes, getting on in years, and it was absolutely terrified.

Barking its lungs out but wagging its tail furiously at the same time, the poor thing knew there was something dreadfully wrong. After days, I didn't know how many, with its beloved Alf dead, no food, no water, it was utterly confused by life, me and the police. This anxious, troubled, tubby little animal wasn't going to hurt anyone.

I shouted to the throng outside that I'd found the biggest and fiercest specimen of the Japanese Mouse Hound ever seen, and called to it in soothing and encouraging tones, feeling in my pocket for my dog lead. A police officer is never without handcuffs; an RSPCA inspector is never without a dog lead. At the sight of mine the terrier, perhaps of the view that leads implied long and strenuous walks over the hills and far away, turned and bolted into the sitting room, where it hid under the chair that Alf was seemingly asleep in. I'd never seen a dead person before. He looked rather grey but otherwise exactly like any bloke who'd had a few pints on a Sunday lunchtime and, after the roast beef and Yorkshire pud, was taking his customary afternoon nap in front of the fire.

I crawled on my knees towards the dog, held it by the collar and pulled it out from under with no resistance. As I stood, keeping the dog firmly in the crook of my arm and stroking it, I heard myself starting to explain to Alf what I was doing and why, and apologising for taking his dog away.

The name on the collar was Buster, and chubby little Buster was still quivering with fright but definitely getting calmer when I walked from the house. As ever, the constables expressed their admiration openly for someone who can deal with a barking dog. They parted before me like the waters of the Red Sea before Moses, or the waters of Whitby harbour before the good ship *Lollipop*. I nodded my acceptance of their esteem, all in a day's work don't you know, and said I'd be back later for the cats.

It was after nine by the time I got to the building designated as the RSPCA dog pound. This was an old lean-to greenhouse and potting shed where, in days gone by, municipal gardeners employed by Scorswick Urban District Council had pricked out their geraniums and transplanted their begonias for the floral clock at the entrance to the park. My inspector predecessor had picked up two mortuary slabs from somewhere, a mortuary I supposed, which he'd set up on sturdy plinths, for the purpose of examining animals and putting them down if he had to. We called it euthanising. The stuff we used, pentobarbitone sodium, trade name Euthatal, gave an animal a humane, painless and quick end but we were still killing it, and we didn't do it without a very, very good reason. I had no expectations of that kind for Buster.

In my shed I only had accommodation for up to three dogs, plus cages and baskets for cats and birds. My dog pound was a staging post only. The Jack Russell and the cats would have to go to York, where we had substantial facilities and where we'd put the animals up for adoption. This would be difficult for Buster, I knew, because of his age, but we'd try our hardest. I went back to Alf's for the cats.

Seeing the inside of the house in daylight was a bit of a shock. It was truly filthy. My shoes stuck to the carpet as I walked and made that squishy, suction noise. And the whole place stank to high heaven of cat pee. My, how it stank. How I'd missed the smell before, I don't know. Must have been the excitement. Anyway, it was as near to overpowering as you could get without actually fainting to the floor. Never mind, I had to get on and find these cats.

I'd been told there were fifteen but I'd brought cat baskets for twenty. I would have to make sure there were no animals left behind and I knew that if there was the tiniest secret hidey-hole inaccessible to an RSPCA man, a cat would find it. In my time I have retrieved cats from up chimneys, under floorboards, behind the skirting, in the airing cupboard, under the kitchen sink. One of my colleagues once had to take the panelling off a bath to get a cat out, and there was absolutely no hint of how a cat could have wriggled in there. Here I was relatively lucky. On the tops of wardrobes and under beds was the extent of it and, after an hour and a half, I was sure I'd got them all, and fifteen it was.

Despite the wintry weather I was sweating buckets when I'd finished, so I threw my jacket and jumper in the back of the van with the last cat and set off for Scorswick in my short-sleeved shirt. I was debating whether to make the trip to York later today or tomorrow as I joined the dual carriageway into town. I flicked the indicator, turned the steering wheel and happened to catch sight of my arms.

You've seen those Tom and Jerry cartoons, where the cat puts his paw in the light socket and the shock makes him do a flying star jump with every hair standing on end, his tongue shooting out, his ears flashing on and off and his eyes whizzing around and around. That was me on the dual carriageway as I saw ten thousand fleas crawling about on my bare skin.

I must have been like a walking oasis when I went into Alf's house, a mobile flea banquet for the starving, and there were so many I could hardly see a patch of myself. I did what I think most people would have done in such a circumstance. I panicked.

In trying to slap both my arms with both my hands at once, my attention strayed from the road. When it strayed back again I saw the rear window and boot of a gold Rolls-Royce about six feet away. I braked of course but it was no good. I clattered right into the back of him. I thought, 'You must not release ten thousand fleas into the environment. Don't get out.' I also thought 'Oh bugger,' as I reversed ten yards and heard the sound of metal parting from metal.

The owner of the Roller got out all right, with some difficulty as he was the wrong shape for sharp movement. He cut more of a portly than a lithe and lissom figure, and very bristly he looked. I watched him stomp towards me and I could see he was no got-rich-quick barrow boy, flashing his wealth with a fancy motor. Rather, he was a retired major general, or a fourteenth earl, or Goldfinger. Those folk unfortunate enough to live in regions other than Yorkshire, and those who know it not, may believe that we're all flat 'ats and whippets and frothy beer, but

I can assure you that we do have gentry, and this was gentry all right.

His chestnut-brown Oxford brogues, polished to that deep lustre only possible with the finest hand-cured leathers, pure beeswax and a valet, thumped the tarmac with the sureness of a thousand years of superior breeding. His gingery Harris tweed suit with waistcoat, possibly a family heirloom but certainly built for posterity by the Indian and Colonial Outfitters, was amply cut, allowing for the largest lunches and the swiftest interchange of double-barrelled shotguns with his loaders.

As he stomped, he waved his arms about and tried to speak, his face suffused in a fairground kind of red, his purple nose pulsating, his moustache and equally hairy eyebrows twitching like three massive caterpillars in spasm. His spitting, frothing fury, and incomprehension of the inexplicable, could not have been greater had the barman at his club told him they were out of Angostura for the pink gin.

His car was, like its driver, a fine example of the species. It was a classic, the sort you could use as a tank if you fitted a cannon to it, with running boards and big headlights on the wings, and my Escort van was bound to have come off much the worse. So what was all the fuss about?

I thought I'd better get out after all. I said I was very sorry and, as he cursed me for a stupid oik of a peasant who should never have been granted access to the Queen's highway but rather exposed on a hillside at birth, he saw me still slapping at my arms. He stopped dead. He peered. I jerked my thumb towards the van side behind me, where was written in large letters 'RSPCA'.

'I've just rescued fifteen cats,' I started to say, 'and the owner had been dead for days. Fleas were starving so they all . . .' but my gentleman with the scratched Rolls-Royce was already backing off, his facial colours modifying to a certain extent, nearer to pastel shades with just a hint of white-not-quite.

His retaking of his driving seat was almost spring-lamb like, and his standing start with added blue smoke would have done credit to Stirling Moss. And I never heard another thing about it.

Rather than explain to my boss that I'd had a collision with a very heavy low-flying bumble bee, I thought I'd get the van fixed myself. I'd have to hope that the owner of the golden Roller wasn't local, and definitely not someone who might one day call the RSPCA because his lady wife's little dog was stuck down a badger sett. But that's another story.

I drove as quickly as was reasonable to my cat and dog rescue centre, the old council potting shed, and installed the cat baskets. Not to worry, I told them. Only a temporary arrangement. I needed to get changed and have a bath. Before setting off home, I sprayed myself with a whole can of Nuvan Top, a highly effective flea killer now taken off the market because it was found to be carcinogenic.

Nearly everything we used in those days has been taken off the market. It's a wonder we're still here.

Being bitten by fleas was an occupational hazard, which was why I hadn't noticed much in the way of itching. The odd flea here and there, fair enough, part and parcel, but now I was standing in a crunchy heap of dead ones and I was quite sure they were no more than the advance party. The rest had yet to emerge from my nooks and crannies. I considered my next move. My wife Carol had to be told. There was no way around it. I stopped at the phone box and rang in.

You see, I said, I need a bath and a change of clothes because of this slight flea problem. No way, matey boy, was Carol's response. I wasn't going in the house covered in fleas. I wasn't going in the house even with one flea that I knew about.

My pleas and entreaties, and appeals to the loving side of her nature, eventually produced a marginal softening in her attitude. A plan was agreed.

Her part of the plan was to run a bath and open the bathroom window (we lived in a bungalow). My part was to strip off on the back lawn in the perishing cold, stuff my socks, shirt and underclothes into an old feed sack ready for burning, leave my RSPCA gear spread out on the grass for dealing with later, and climb in through the bathroom window. I could see Carol looking out from the kitchen as I did all this, smiling, with a cup of tea in her hand and a piece of curd tart.

The bath was hot and foaming. Carol had dissolved half a bottle of car shampoo in it. I slid in and watched with some satisfaction as a layer of dead fleas formed in the suds. I pulled the plug, to get rid of this bath-load and start again with another, and the sheer volume of bodies clogged the plughole. I pushed them down with a nailbrush and, the bath clean, ran another tub of hot water.

There were hardly any fleas left now, no more than a hundred or so. I sank back and relaxed, and remembered an old story about how a fox is supposed to get rid of his fleas. He goes to a barbed wire fence, grabs a bunch of sheep's wool in his mouth then jumps in the river. As he swims up and down, his fleas run along his nose to what they think will be a better berth on a sheep and, at the right moment, he says goodbye.

I too said goodbye as I pulled the plug and called to Carol that the delousing process was complete. While she'd watched me earlier through the kitchen window, she hadn't only been enjoying my come-uppance from my beloved animals that always came first in our lives. She had also noticed that I had acquired approximately three million flea bites and that my body appeared to have been drained of blood.

She came into the bathroom spraying Nuvan Top before her and carrying a large bottle of calamine lotion, with which she began dabbing. Well, there wasn't much of me left undabbed but what there was did credit to the cleansing powers of car shampoo. Even when I was mostly covered with fresh clothes and RSPCA uniform, my face and neck were still visible, skin of a deathly pallor liberally blotched with the crusty pinkish chalk of dried calamine.

Carol told me I should take the rest of the day off, having first burned my undergarments in the garden incinerator, sprayed my van and sprayed the uniform in the garden before hanging it on the line, there to stay through several nights of January frost until we could be sure all wildlife therein had been extinguished.

I did as I was told except for the day off bit. There were no SOS messages, for a change, so I was able to take the cats and Buster to York, where I was the source of much amusement and the inspiration for a series of imaginative and comical remarks which would run and run and never quite fade away. My fleas would be a feature of every Christmas do for years to come.

Shirley, the girl on the desk, reminded me of someone. Marianne Faithfull? Mary Hopkin? She sang a song especially for me, an old song by The Coasters called 'Poison Ivy'.

'It's gonna take an ocean, dum-de-dum-de-dum, of calamine lotion. You'll be scratchin' like a hound, the minute she starts to mess around.' Yes, yes, very funny.

I was fading as fast as the daylight as I drove home, feeling feverish, sweating but shivering with cold, and aching all over. I thought I must be coming down with flu but Carol had other ideas. She sent me to bed and called the doctor.

This doctor, quite unlike the breezy young woman earlier, was one of the old school, the sort who arrives in a dinner jacket if you call him out at night. He thought my story most entertaining and had no difficulty with his diagnosis: blood poisoning.

'I have known very severe cases,' he said, gravely, 'where limbs have had to be amputated. In extremis, you understand. Another aspect of the presentation can be boils. Yes, you might come out in boils. If you do, I shall have to lance them, of course.'

Carol has always denied telling this doctor to wind me up but I don't think she would have missed such a golden opportunity.

Despite having made his diagnosis, he went around the houses again with another examination. Pulse, stethoscope, torch thing for looking in your ears and eyes, thermometer.

'Hm,' he said. 'Hm.' He began to pack his bag.

'Doctor?' was all I could manage.

'Ah, yes, Mr Langdale. Thing is, you see, I am not entirely convinced that your particular case would be best served by the modern treatment of antibiotics. I rather think the old traditional cure might be best. Yes. I think so. In your case.'

'Traditional cure?' I asked, thinking of leeches, or perhaps blood-letting.

'Large doses of quinine and whisky. Half a bottle of whisky a day, for a week, should do the trick, plus quinine tablets dissolved in hot milk. I'll instruct Mrs Langdale. Good evening to you.'

I had no strength to complain and sank into the pillows in despair. Amputations? Boils? A week? How could I take a week off? And what was Carol going to say about the cost of all that whisky? I didn't suppose she could go to the off-licence with a doctor's prescription and ask for a free half-dozen of VAT 69.

I heard the front door go and the sound of the kettle being put on. A few minutes later, Carol came in with some hot lemon and honey and two small white pills.

'Marvellous,' she said, keeping her face perfectly straight. 'These modern antibiotics. So much power in a tiny tablet. Thank the Lord for medical science, that's what I say. Two now, two every four hours thereafter.' I swallowed the pills and washed them down with hot lemon. 'You'll be all right for work the day after tomorrow, and completely all right by the end of a week. Only thing with these pills is – no alcohol.'

The police, the police surgeon and the ambulance men who came to pick up Alf's body, all complained about having a couple of flea bites but nobody thanked me for taking almost the entire swarm away with me. Social services had to fumigate the house twice before anyone would go in it again. York office found homes for all the cats and, after three months, an elderly couple who had lost their own dog offered to take Buster, so my first big job in my new world had had a happy ending, as I repeatedly told myself while hoping that none of my more athletic fleas had managed the leap from me to his lordship's gingery Harris tweed suit.

2

WHEN I WERE A LAD

Fleas or no fleas, being an RSPCA inspector seemed to me the perfect job, as if I'd been born to it, which I must have been because I can't remember a time when I wasn't fascinated by animals.

Where I grew up (in the fishing town of Hull, close to the docks) and when (in the 1960s), nobody thought anything of kids roaming free. I don't quite know how my mother decided when I was old enough to go out alone, but the minute she did I was off and away. Had I been able to range across the Serengeti I would doubtless have marvelled at the big exciting animals but probably missed the detail. As my range was somewhat more confined, being the old railway sidings by the docks, I uncovered all sorts of details, like rare flowers, butterflies and beetles.

Great crested newts, or horse newts as we called them, were quite hard to find then but I knew where they were.

I soon expanded my territory to the streams, woods, open country, hedgerows and, of course, the sea. It was fifteen miles to Spurn Point and it took all day to walk there and back, but that didn't matter. Lizards lived there. A bit nearer, between Hornsea and Withernsea, was Aldbrough, where there'd been a bombing range during the war. Some of the clusters of bomb craters had turned into ponds, and wherever there's a pond there's a whole world of life to find. There, I could see grass snakes, and dragonflies, and gather frogspawn to hatch at home, and collect live daphnia for my fish tank.

I had friends, too, young adventurers and explorers like me, who were interested in the things that lived in ponds and woods but they weren't as interested as I was. We were all happy doing our Just William thing, roving about the countryside and along the seashore but, unlike William Brown, my mates also liked to play cricket and football in the street, or go to watch Hull KR play rugby league. I wasn't against any of that. I joined in, but with me, the priority was the wildlife. The exploits of F. S. Trueman and D. B. Close held a certain fascination that was soon overtaken by the problems of catching a certain eel, with which I'd become acquainted by staring for hours on end into a stream.

All this meant that I really only had two reliable companions. One was our dog, Skipper, who did have some of that archetypal Yorkshire canine in him, being part whippet and part a lot else besides, and the other was Brian. Anyone who has seen the film *Kes* has seen Brian, the pale, skin-and-bone, out-of-place raggedy boy, except Brian's scruffy head had blond hair growing out of it. Brian's large family had no visible means of support and so, without our modern social security system, they had nothing at all. If I ever grumbled about lack of generosity in the pocket-money department, I was invited to exchange my paltry income for whatever Brian or any of his half-dozen siblings might be on. Or, instead of our handing down our old clothes and anything else useful to Brian's lot, we could reverse the flow of trade.

Although slightly wealthier than Brian, I still felt the urge to increase my stock, and one of the ways I did it was by dealing in pigeon futures. Quite a few of us had lofts and we'd race between ourselves, and occasionally we'd find ourselves in possession of a possible contender. Even more occasionally, a real pigeon fancier, one who raced for money, might pay us something well below market value for such a bird, but our best customer was Mrs Atkinson.

We were all terrified of Mrs Atkinson. She had a face like a herring gull and a voice to match. She could slice wedding cakes at a hundred yards with that voice. When we had to read *Macbeth* at school, there in all our minds instantly were three Mrs Atkinsons in the opening scene, and when we went to see *The Wizard of Oz*, there she was again, the Wicked Witch of the West.

Mrs Ack didn't have a pigeon loft. She didn't race pigeons. She just kept them. The walls of her back yard and part of the outside of the house were decorated in the manner of a loft, in stripes of dark green and white paint to help the birds find their way home, but they were not kept in at all. They sat around, perched on every available inch of space, cooing and chuckling, and Mrs Ack presided, feeding them royally.

If something surprised them, they'd take off in a great clatter, a cloud of pigeons wheeling about the sky, and then they'd return, pushing each other off window sills and guttering until all were settled once more.

There was a mystery about Mrs Atkinson and her pigeons. She never refused to buy from us, at a threepenny bit per bird, yet her population seemed to remain constant. Yet, she claimed no pigeon ever flew from her care because of her unique discovery as regards homing instincts. By experiment and intellectual endeavour, she had found that three minutes was the ideal time for her to hold a pigeon's head in her mouth, lips closed around its neck. These special minutes removed all primitive desires to wander and made Mrs Ack's back yard the pigeon's magnetic home, sweet home.

We also observed her holding the heads of certain birds under the cold tap, for three minutes by her watch. These were ones that she could tell in advance would not respond properly to the mouth treatment and so needed their brains washing 'like the Chinese do'. Neither the Chinese nor the mouth method ever worked for us, possibly because we didn't have the knack of telling which bird should have which, and we were reduced to the orthodox way of developing a homing response by keeping new birds locked up for a few weeks.

So, if Mrs Ack's birds never deserted her but their numbers stayed at the same yard-filling maximum despite our constant additions, there could only be one conclusion. Pigeon pie. That such an awe-inspiring old hag could be telling us lies never occurred. It had to be pigeon pie, or possibly she used some of them in spells.

Anyway, this was the marketing end of our business. The production side was much more risky, not financially, because there were no costs, but personally. Our source of supply was the massive flock of retired racing pigeons and descendants thereof that lived in among the heavy timbers of the old jetties by the docks. These pigeons, without the benefit of Mrs Ack's Chinese treatments, had fled their former owners, or their ancestors had, and become feral. They bred and bred, at all times of year, and the import-export trade in grain and other foodstuffs through the port of Kingston upon Hull gave them plenty to eat at every season.

Our target was the squabs, the near-fledged but not flying, sitting in the nest waiting for the journey of life to begin. Brian and I would walk along the jetty decks, peering through the gaps in the planks to find a suitable nest. When we did, Brian would stay there while I ran back to the shore. Brian was my navigation beacon. His shouts guided me to himself and the nest. My route depended on the state of the tide.

If it was out, I could stay at a low level, climbing along the jetty beams, which meant I wouldn't have far to fall into the mud below, thus reducing my chances of disappearing entirely as I hit the fathomless slop. The downside was that the beams were wet and covered in seaweed, shellfish and slime, all very slippery.

If the tide was in I was forced up much higher and had to start my route a lot further away, but the beams were relatively hazardless. I didn't really mind the thought of falling in the water in any case. I was a good swimmer, but nobody wanted to end up in that mud.

For me, the task of getting there and getting back with a shirtful of wriggling squabs was the most satisfying thing I knew. For Brian, shivering up above on a wintry Hull day with my cast-off shirt to keep him warm, the only reward was the threepenny bits and he didn't seem to care much about them.

Come the spring and I would be in the woods, continuing my studies of miracles. One day I was up a tree, looking into a blackbird's nest, checking that Mr and Mrs B had not been neglecting their duties and that all six of their offspring were thriving. These chicks were almost ready to step out onto the branches to try their wings. I didn't want to stay long in case I put the parents off but the sound of footfalls below made me hesitate.

Oh no. It was Johnny Edwards, known as Eddie, a boy two years above me at school and one to keep clear of. He was big for his age, therefore much bigger than me, and he was feared for his ability to thump the living daylights out of anyone he cared to take on. If a foolish new boy came to school with a lunch box, Eddie would demand to know what was in it. He'd take a bite of a sandwich, spit it out in disgust, and smack the boy about for trying to poison him. I hoped that if I stayed still in my tree, he wouldn't notice me, but he saw my faithful Skipper sitting at the bottom, looking up.

'What's in t'nest?' he shouted.

'Nowt,' I called back.

'Get down here,' he replied. Thinking about the alternatives, I did what he said.

'What's in t'nest?' he said again.

'No eggs,' I said. 'Only blackbird chicks.' He had a duffel bag, its cord drawn tight shut, which he placed gently against the tree trunk. I noted the gently, and wondered.

'Don't touch,' was his economic instruction, with the death threat left unspoken, as he shinned up the tree to reach inside the nest, stuff the chicks in his jacket pockets, and slide down again.

The next thing was doubly amazing: to see what was in the duffel bag, and to have proof that Eddie was human all at the same time. Even though I represented to him a matter of no more importance than a dead amoeba, his pride in his duffel bag's contents was such that I became an audience. He loosened the cord carefully, and slowly reached inside. I could hear a very odd noise, quite loud, like two wooden rulers being tapped together in anger.

So far, it looked to me like a magician pulling a rabbit out of a hat. This was Eddie's showy variation, pulling his trained pet clicking rabbit out of his duffel bag, but instead of a rabbit he drew forth a ball of feathers, brown and grey. I knew immediately what it was although it was the first time I'd seen one. I had pictures at home in my animal books. It was a young tawny owl.

The tawny is the most common British owl, about fifteen inches tall with a wingspan over three feet. It's the one that allegedly says *tu-whit tu-whoo*, although what it actually says is either something like *kerwick*, or something like *hoo-hoo*, and if you hear both it's two owls calling, probably a male and a female. It has a rather rotund appearance and a serious manner, and the young ones have more grey feathers on their heads and upper bodies so they look like miniature high-court judges in full wig.

This judge seemed rather narked, making its angry ruler noises with its beak and digging its talons into Eddie's arm. Whatever its expectations when out of the bag, things clearly were not happening quickly enough. Eddie took the hint and a chick from his pocket. The owl put its head back and opened wide. In went the chick, not very much smaller than the owl's head, wig included. After two gulps, all that was visible of the chick was one skinny leg dangling out of the owl's closed beak. Another swallow and that was gone too.

I felt my eyes so big and popping that I must have looked like an owl myself. I don't think I'd drawn a breath through the whole proceedings. I knew from Sunday School about St Paul and his blinding vision on the road to Damascus. This was my Damascene moment. Whatever else might happen in my life and whatever obstacles might lie in my way, one thing was sure and certain. I had to have an owl.

When Eddie pulled another owlet out of his bag and fed it too, my owl-owning necessity suddenly had ways and means. He didn't want two. One would be mine. I asked Eddie if I could come with him to find more owl food. He shrugged. I could if I wanted.

By the end of that day I had made my calculations and my decision. With my savings, next week's pocket money and a major initiative on Mrs Atkinson, I could raise about six shillings.

'I'll give you ten bob for one of them owls,' I said, almost fainting with the excitement and what the City slickers call the exposure. Ten shillings was a colossal amount, and I didn't have it. Eddie was too clever for me. He could recognise sheer desperation, and shook his head.

'Five shillings and my fishing rod.' How pathetic, said Eddie's snort. 'All right. My fishing rod, reel and tackle included, five shillings, and a two-shilling book token.' The book token, Eddie well knew, could be exchanged at the newsagent's for ten cigarettes, normal price one and tenpence.

Eddie picked up his duffel bag, slung it over his shoulder, and walked away. It was the classic salesman's manoeuvre. If you really want someone to buy, tell him he can't have it. I walked home so slowly, I'm surprised I got there before bedtime.

'I'm not keeping tea things out all night in case you turn up, our Carter,' said my mother. 'There's bread and cheese in the pantry. And you can give some to that dog who's been out all day with nothing.'

I lay awake in bed, trying to make owls seem less essential than life itself, and failing. No, there was nothing for it. A boy had to do what a boy had to do, and the condemned boy ate a hearty breakfast very fast. Round at Eddie's house, I knocked on the door. He answered.

'My fishing rod and tackle, my new rugby ball, five shillings and my sheath knife.' Eddie almost smiled. Maybe he'd be a professional torturer when he left school.

'My fishing rod and tackle, my new rugby ball, five shillings, my sheath knife . . .' and here I had to pause. This was to be a pledge of galactic proportions. I was about to offer Eddie the one object I prized above all else: '. . . and my air pistol. Webley. Point one seven seven.'

'With a tin of slugs. And that book token,' said a cool Eddie.

I nodded. I was now destitute. I had endowed Eddie with all my worldly goods. He must have known I had nothing left and had driven me until I could be driven no further. But, joy of joys, I had my owl.

I ran home, got all the money out of my pot pig, ran to the ironmonger's, bought a tin of slugs, ran home again, picked up my rod, rugby ball, fishing bag and all, and ran to Eddie's. With all the drama of two spies being exchanged at Checkpoint Charlie, I swapped my entire wealth for a funny little heap of feathers. I had never been so happy. I was home in a fraction of a second and moving pigeons from one loft to another so that My Owl could have his own spacious apartment.

He was not appreciative. He clicked and complained like mad at the indignity of his recent imprisonment inside a blue cotton bag with Yorkshire Penny Bank written on it, and he looked around with suspicion in his gaze. Where, he wanted to know, was his breakfast? And his lunch, come to that? My mother had some stewing steak she was going to make into a pie for our tea, so I begged a little lump of that, wrapped it in a few small pigeon feathers, and down it went.

Such a dietary regimen couldn't last, of course – or could it? Mother soon had the butcher saving unconsidered bits and pieces and Tal didn't seem to mind if it was beef, lamb or pork or what cut it was, although there was an overall preference for chicken. The feathers were for roughage, to maintain his natural system, which includes making pellets of indigestibles and regurgitating them.

My family had had all sorts of suggestions for a name

but I stuck to Tal, short for talons, seeing as he had extra large ones. It was a boring name, but I'd thought of it, so there. A couple of weeks passed and Tal started flapping about, seeming to want more space, so I went to the library and got a book out about falconry. There were drawings of various tools of the trade and I copied one of the less ornamental pictures of jesses. A jess is a two-piece leather strap which fits around the bird's leg, normally to be attached to a training line or the falconer's glove by means of a swivel. I didn't have a swivel so I used a key ring, and I didn't have any leather so I used the canvas from an old plimsoll, and the idea was not training but to give Tal the freedom of our yard on a running line.

He seemed pleased about this and made a certain place on the back wall his own, where he'd sit and watch the world go by, bobbing up and down and turning his head through something like 270 degrees. Celebrity status followed. The coalman, the bin men and the milkman all brought titbits for Tal. My mother, returning from shopping, would find Tal swooping down with a screech to land on her basket, and he wouldn't let go until she gave him a scrap of chicken or whatever. Everybody in the neighbourhood came to look, and he grew and he grew.

I was grateful for the butcher's meat but concerned that it wasn't really the proper thing for an owl whose diet in the wild would mainly be small furry rodents, young birds when there were any, and the occasional frog or fish. They hunt mainly at night, not with especially good eyesight but, as owls do, with exceptional hearing. They're about ten times better than us at hearing low-frequency sounds, as a little vole might make when moving through the grass, and their ears are not symmetrically placed on their heads, so the very slight differences in each ear's reception is computed by the brain to give them superior ability to tell where sounds are coming from.

Worms and beetles too are part of the wild diet but when I tried a worm on Tal he gave me a distinctly funny look, as one would if one was used to *poulet à la mode* and *collet d'agneau*. And so it was that I became a martyr to a never-ending task.

Each morning I'd be up long before anyone else, slurping a high-speed bowl of cornflakes and trotting the mile and a half to my original wildlifing range, the old railway sidings. I had twelve mousetraps in my system. I set six, usually with a piece of sweet biscuit as bait, and collected the six from the day before. These went into my satchel and the catch into my school-blazer pockets, two, three or sometimes four small rodents, shrews and voles mostly. The traps would have to be cleaned at home that night, and fumigated. Wild rodents will not touch a trap that smells of blood. They sense it, not like house mice. So I used to dangle the traps one at a time on a toasting fork, over the smoke from the coal fire, and that got rid of the taint.

Beyond my trapping grounds was a timber yard, and beyond that a goods railway line from the docks. A train would come along at the same time each day and slow down for a certain junction, allowing me to leap on it and cadge a lift almost all the way to school. If I ran the last half-mile at top speed, I could just slip in before the bell.

My system was hard work but worthwhile, and my predations on the local rodent population seemed to be sustainable. Tal was growing into a feisty adult and a real character but his fame had not, apparently, spread into the masters' common room at my school. Everybody in my class knew about my trapping except our form teacher, who ordered a search of satchels and pockets after an announcement in assembly about a sudden rush of petty thefts. I was most reluctant to turn out mine, so our master nominated me as prime suspect. Towering over me, he thrust a hand into each side pocket. I can see his face now. Expecting to find someone's fountain pen or several lots of dinner money, he instead felt something cold, furry and damp.

He felt again, couldn't believe what his fingers were telling him, so pulled out two dead shrews. Destroying his credibility with that class in one instant, he squealed, went white, dropped the shrews on the floor, and left the room. I picked the bodies up, put them back in my pockets, enjoyed my few minutes as class hero, and looked forward to a search-free summer.

My vole harvest began to thin out. I was, eventually, having the same effects on the small rodents of that part of Hull as the rainforest loggers have on the tree dwellers of the Amazon. Of course I didn't see it that way. All I could think about was alternative means of supply, which meant ranging further and wider, which meant getting up earlier and earlier and finding myself later and later for school. I was in a difficult position, being permanently skint but needing to buy in. My only option was to trade and, after my deal with Eddie, I had precious little to trade with.

Each week I could pay pennies for road-kill and various things shot by air-gun owners, until the pocket money ran out. After that I only had my museum, a collection of shells and oddities kept in four shoe boxes, which was hardly a big come-on apart from some of the fossils I'd found on trips to Whitby, and my bird's egg collection.

Being left with nothing forced me to recognise an uncomfortable fact. Tal was from the wild and he needed to go back. If further proof were needed it came one night when I heard another owl answering his calls. Tal was *tu-whitting* and the other was *tu-whooing*. Next night I stayed up to watch and saw another tawny on a house roof opposite. To my utter amazement, it flew down and perched beside Tal on our wall, and they carried on calling to each other.

This was in a back street in Hull, with not a tree in sight, and here was a wild female tawny owl trying to get off with the tame male. There was only one way to resolve the matter, and the next time she came to sit on the roof, I released Tal from his bonds. Straight away he flew up to join his mate, and there they were, *whitting* and *whooing* on the ridge tiles. Such birds, I knew, mate for life, and would set up a territory somewhere and defend it against other owls, and their young against all-comers.

I thought that would be the last I'd see of them as they flew away, but they were back the next night looking for chicken. I threw what meat I could get, and dead mice, onto the roof and it was three months before they stopped coming.

By the time I was fifteen, nearing school-leaving age, with Tal long gone and my pigeon loft no longer such a fascinating place, Mrs Atkinson in a home and Brian disappeared out of my life, I was like the Cisco Kid without a Pancho. I had a bike, I had a .22 air rifle that I could strap to the crossbar, and every weekend and school holiday to hunt, shoot, fish and look.

On Saturday mornings, my favourite was to bike to Hessle where there was (and still is) a park cum nature reserve called Little Switzerland. There were made paths through the trees and gravelled walks for leisurely strollers but I got right off the beaten track, heading always first for the chalk pits. These were old limestone quarries, a piece of the edge of the Wolds become a set of natural ponds rich in all manner of creatures and plants.

On this particular morning the trees were in their full spring leaf, the sun was bright in a blue sky and my own private wildlife sanctuary was busy. You could sit perfectly still and sense it – optimism, new life, growth, everything dashing about on a mission. I had my gun. I was Langdale of the Jungle, making my way silently across uncharted territory, listening for the crack of a twig which might betray the presence of the deadly Uckawi tribe, headhunters of Hessle and District.

What I did hear was silence; then, striking the air with a purity never found in any orchestra, a song thrush. He ran through his repertoire of single notes, warbles and riffs, then did it all again, and again. I could see him, on a branch of a beech tree, high up, telling me and anyone else within earshot that there was nothing, but nothing, better to do on a fine spring morning in England than to sing his finest song. What happened in the next few seconds is a blank in my mind. I wish the rest of it was a blank too, but it isn't.

The song stopped and the bird tumbled from the tree. A few tiny feathers floated in the space where he'd been and began their slow zigzag down, in and out of the shafts of sunlight, while their former wearer's fall was halted in some branches a few feet off the ground. I threw my gun aside and swiftly made the few steps to the beech tree. As I reached it, the gods of the forest shook those branches and the dead thrush dropped at my feet.

I looked at it. I could see one eye half closed. After maybe a minute I made myself pick it up, a warm, damp bundle of nothing with two teardrops of fresh blood on its chest. Moments before, it had been singing the hymn of life. I cannot begin to tell how horrible I felt.

I could have dropped to my knees and begged forgiveness, or sighed and sobbed over the death of poor cock robin. Instead I threw the body into a pond and made a simple promise to myself, that I would never, ever, do anything like that again as long as I lived.

3

THE ELECTROPHANATOR
AND ME

After leaving school I had a brief dab at the navy, a sojourn chiefly remembered for the happy hours spent cleaning the bogs with a toothbrush. That was followed by half a year trying every job on every postcard pinned up at the Hull Labour Exchange. I attempted to explain to my father why it was that I appeared to be so useless. It wasn't that I was, actually, useless; it was because I really was keen to work with animals.

'You want to try cousin Jack,' said my dad.

'Cousin Jack? Who's he?' said I, knowing my dad's sense of humour and so imagining that this previously unmentioned relative was perhaps a lonely goatherd living in a cave on the Lincolnshire Wolds, or someone who reared goldfish for the funfairs.

'RSPCA, is our Jack. Has been as long as I can remember. Tell him that your mother's mother's sister was his wife's brother's wife, or something of the sort. Put that kettle on as you go.'

Quite how this information had passed me by I couldn't explain, but cousin Jack, Jack Hartley, turned out to be an RSPCA senior figure, manager of the Hull station, and had been with the firm for thirty years. By this time he was approaching retirement with no enthusiasm for that indolent state at all. He was the big, bluff type, what you see is what you get, the sort who had respect for higher authority but no need of it and – not always visibly or obviously – would do anything to help anyone. Maybe such people still exist.

I called 'our Jack' from one of the special cream-painted Hull phone boxes and started to tell him about his sisters and his cousins and his aunts, but he seemed to know who I was anyway and told me to pop down and see him. Later I found out that he wasn't a cousin at all but somebody Dad knew from the pub.

'Now then, young Master Langdale,' he said, after crushing my right hand into a third of its normal size, 'sit you down and I'll tell you what it is. The girl's leaving to run after one of them long-haired boys that plays a banjo on the stage, and we've never had a lad doing it. But that doesn't mean we won't.' I tried to look hopeful and expectant, rather than stupid. If I listened carefully, I thought, I might be able to divine what on earth he was on about.

'Twenty kennels,' he continued. 'Sometimes up to twenty dogs, but never more. Understand?' I nodded, hoping he wouldn't test me. 'If there's no room when a new dog comes in, and we have to make room, you see, with the electrophanator, no blame can be attached to the kennel maid or, in this case, the kennel knave I suppose you are. Even so, if it was me, I'd regard it as a personal failure. Now, let's go and have a look.'

Electro what? Cousin Jack pronounced this new word 'electro-FANter-nor'. By the time I found out what it was, I would know it was an ee-lec-TROFFernater. Meanwhile, I had wild pictures in my mind of a dog-eating electrophant, pictures based on a boyhood trip to Scarborough where, in Northstead Manor Gardens, they'd had a gaudily painted mechanical elephant with castors on its feet, which gave small children rides in its howdah.

There were indeed twenty concrete cells, or holding pens, for stray dogs. As we walked along the barred fronts, every one of the inmates came rushing up, tail wagging, wanting whatever it was we might have, hoping that we might represent something better than their clean, tidy, all-essentials-catered-for lives, which were, nevertheless, awful for a dog.

'For every miserable, sinful bastard who abandons a dog, or mistreats a dog, there has to be a person of the opposite kind, who will take this dog in and give it love and care and respect,' said our Jack.

I was right with it now. I was to be employed by the

RSPCA to look after the kennels and the strays and keep all in as good a condition as possible, and the better I did my job, the more likely it would be that a citizen of Hull and environs would find one of my charges attractive enough to take home. I smiled. Goodbye, Labour Exchange. Hello, destiny.

*

A large part of the work was mucky and repetitive. I had to scrub out twice a day and all my guests had to be fed, watered and exercised. That much was set in stone but it didn't take up all my hours. New dogs usually needed some extra attention, which was no problem, and in any time spare from my routines I was happy fooling around with all the dogs. Some of them clearly had never had even the most basic training. Some had never known the fun a dog can have, just by being a dog with a kind and caring human. Some distrusted humans entirely, and winning their trust was a kind of emotional torture because I knew the original distrust might eventually prove to be well placed, because here came the hard part.

The longer-term residents created special pressures. As the numbers mounted in the kennels – seventeen, eighteen, nineteen – it became more and more important to persuade the nice people who came looking for a rescue dog that the one nobody had wanted so far, the one in kennel nineteen, was the one they should have. If not, and of course this had to remain unsaid, the next dog in would put nineteen into twenty, and there was no twenty-one, only The End.

My powers of persuasion, I felt, were not as fully developed as they might have been. I read a book called *How to Win Friends and Influence People*. No use at all. I tried smooth-talking charm, but I never was cut out to be an estate agent. I tried little white lies, funny stories made up to make the less appealing hounds seem to be jolly characters, despite their shortage of good looks. I can't say it worked very often. Something clicks between dog and potential owner, or it doesn't. Even so, I could never give up, and I never could become immune to what our Jack had called 'a personal failure'.

As kennel knave, I was mostly enjoying myself but it wasn't what you might call a career position. I'd made my way into the RSPCA but at the very bottom, and I was looking for a step up. The most obvious, and the most exciting, had one big obstacle in the way.

A few of the staff were designated animal ambulance drivers. They had a duty rota, so many nights on call, so many not. If an animal was hurt in a road accident or needed care after any kind of incident, the RSPCA vehicle would attend. This was an idea I fancied, and one of the drivers had left. I'd still be kennel knave in the day but I'd be the RSPCA man at night, out there, in the world, driving to emergencies.

The obstacle was that I couldn't drive. I had a brother-in-law who was sometimes persuaded by my big sister to take me out in his car but I needed practice, lots of it, and some proper lessons if only I had any money to pay for them.

At the age of seventeen, with nothing to declare but my ambition, I applied for the vacancy. When Jack raised the matter of my driving, I told him I'd booked some time off next week to take my test, and my only worry was the Highway Code questions. Jack told me to get swotting and not play with the dogs so much.

I couldn't get my real test booked for another eight weeks so I did the obvious thing. I backed myself to pass first time, and told Jack that I had. He was so pleased that he never asked to see my licence, nor did the police, the fire brigade or anyone else who called me out over the next eight weeks, which gave me the driving practice I needed so that I won my bet with myself and passed the driving test.

Meanwhile, I met a drop-dead gorgeous blonde called Carol. I may have been a little naive but I actually thought that a penniless male kennel maid, whose idea of a good time was sitting up all night on the dockside waiting for a family of foxes to come out, stood a chance with a girl like that. Maybe it was the unpredictability that attracted her. She was expecting the cinema, chicken chow mein and a pound box of Black Magic chocolates. She got six penn'orth of chips and a ride in a small orange box of a van to rescue a cat.

The Hull RSPCA district was without an out-in-the-field inspector at this time, so a locum was brought in, and he would live in the flat above our office. He drove into the yard in his blue van and got out. Now, I had never seen an inspector before, and what I saw seemed like a vision. The uniform was like the police had, with smart tunic and cap, with RSPCA insignia and two silver pips on the shoulders, and I knew instantly that I'd seen my future.

The next weeks only made me more and more determined, as I got to know the man – only a few years older than me – and heard what he did and saw all the kit he had inside his van. He seemed like a free agent, responsible for solving every problem that came up, the dawn-to-dusk patrol, and that just had to be me.

My life now was entirely mapped out. My next job would be as an RSPCA uniformed inspector, and I wanted no more than that for ever and a day, and my companion along life's rocky road would be Carol. There were several things wrong with this map. There could be no question of our getting hitched without the inspector's job. Inspectors got a decent wage, a van to use whenever, and, above all, a house, but the minimum age for inspectors was twenty-two and I was only eighteen.

Time went by, then the good news. They lowered the age for inspectors to twenty. The bad news was that Jack retired, his place as manager was taken by Janet the assistant manager, and her place was taken by Herbert the senior supervisor, a man who hated all living creatures but especially cats, dogs and RSPCA ambulance drivers of whom he had previously been in charge.

Herbert and I did not get on. I could not understand what he was doing there and I must have made that apparent because he designated me as a special case. While maintaining his general dislike of anything that breathed, he never missed an opportunity to stick his knife into me, and a good one came up with his promotion.

'Well, now, good morning young man,' he said to me one day, his white-coated tongue slipping and sliding over his yellow, protruding teeth (he was an ugly sod as well as being so unpleasant). 'I understand you're applying to become an inspector.'

'So I am,' I said, smelling all sorts of large, long-tailed grey rodents.

'I'm the assistant manager now,' said Herbert, in such a way that suggested I should perhaps kneel and offer him an annual tribute of gold, silver and nubile maidens. As I failed to react correctly, he continued. 'One of the assistant manager's jobs, which is always done by the assistant manager, is to write the employment references. So when head office comes calling, asking for a reference for you, I shall have to write it. See?'

I certainly did see, and that future I had planned, with house, van, salary and Carol, vanished like my dad's favourite proverbial substance, Scotch mist. I was devastated. Carol, bless her, did not come up with alternatives, such as my being apprenticed to a painter and decorator, or taking a position as an on-street sales executive with the Hull *Daily Mail*. Her view was that I would win through despite the best efforts of Hateful Herbert, but whether I would have done so without an exceptionally hairy dog, I don't know.

This dog had been brought in to be put down straight away and, as ever, Herbert had volunteered to see to it. I saw him go into the little single-storey building set aside for the purpose, leading an animal I'd never seen the like of. It was massive and hairy beyond belief, like something out of a Hammer horror film. I supposed it was an Alsatian, perhaps crossed with something else such as a water buffalo, but it was one hell of a dog anyway.

Inside the building was the machine used in those days for putting animals down, the electrophanator. It sounds horrifying now but it was the technology of the time. It consisted of a box, an electrical transformer, and some crocodile clips on wires. You put the animal in the box, secured it with collar and leather thong, then attached the clips, one to each ear and one to a back leg.

There were two switches. The first delivered a shock through the animal's brain, knocking it out cold. The second shock stopped the heart. If it sounds like execution by electric chair, it really wasn't as bad as that. If it worked properly, it was as humane a method as we could have had then.

Things were not working properly for Herbert, though, with the hairy timber wolf. Shouts and curses were coming out of the killing shed, so I went in to see what was up. Really I had no business in there but it was on the way to the store cupboard where my stuff for cleaning out the kennels was. Herbert stopped cursing when I went in but I soon saw what was the matter. He'd got the dog in the box all right, and it was tied, although its head was out. As he approached with the crocodile clips the dog gave the most threatening and chilling growl. If Herbert put his hand anywhere near, he could expect to become eligible for disability benefit.

I had to smile at the thought as I headed for the store cupboard, but that little bit of amusement disappeared when I heard the dog cry out. I turned to look and there was Herbert with a length of four-by-two in his hands, about to whack the dog again. I ran over, shouting. If he did that once more, he would feel the four-by-two around his own earholes and might well experience new sensations in his private parts in connection with crocodile clips.

I was taller than him, younger and fitter, and so angry that Herbert could tell I was capable of doing what I said and more.

'All right, then,' he said. 'If you're so ****ing clever, ****head. You do it.'

This was against regulations. I wasn't trained, I wasn't qualified, and I'd never done it. Such thoughts could not enter my crowded brain, (a) because I wanted to spare the dog any more hurt, (b) because I was furious at Herbert, and (c) because I expected the dog to bite my hand off.

The animal seemed to trust me more than it had Herbert, and let me put the clips on its ears. Herbert meanwhile was making a big deal of attaching the last clip to the back leg. We stood back. Herbert threw the first switch.

We were expecting an alive dog to become unconscious, but quite the reverse happened. A quiet dog became mad, in all senses of the word. Screaming its wrath, it translated into a bucking bronco and began wrecking the electrophanator from the inside. The box, something about the size of a trap at a greyhound track, disintegrated before our eyes. The lid flew this way, the back door flew that way, and all the while the dog was howling, and it wasn't the moon it was howling for.

Herbert ran from the room and banged the door shut behind him. I was rooted, unable to move as the hairy monster managed to hurl itself and the box onto the floor, where it burst open completely. The giant was free, and looking for revenge.

There was nothing in the room except another table like the one the electrophanator had been on. I jumped onto it and squatted on my haunches, watching wolfie padding around. He seemed even bigger somehow. Maybe he had a demonic spirit that fed on electricity.

Never in my life before had I been frightened of, or by, an animal. This was a new experience which, as the hound saw me and came my way, I felt would be a last as well as a first.

I didn't know whether to try saying 'Sit!' in a

commanding manner, or 'Nice doggy, good boy' in conciliation, but it didn't matter because my mouth was so dry that I couldn't say anything. All right, Carter, I thought, as the dog tensed, ready to pounce. I hope Carol will still like me with my throat torn out.

The dog reared up on its hind legs. I was motionless, still squatting, all sensations suspended other than fear. It put its enormous front paws on the table, one on either side of me, sniffed my face, and licked me.

Although it had been officially condemned, it had committed no greater crime than appearing to have no owner. It took me two days to find a family who would take it on and, while I was persuading Janet the manager to let me try to do that, I mentioned the matter of my reference and Horrible Herbert. That's all right, she said. He's new to that job. Never done one before. I'll show him how.

4

AN INSPECTOR BOILS

One of the hardest parts of becoming an RSPCA inspector was getting on the training course in the first place. The courses were run every six months and there were thousands of applicants, many of them ex-military, who tended to find favour with the hierarchy who were themselves largely from the same source. There were no female inspectors then, so the whole recruitment culture was biased that way.

My first hurdle would be to avoid my application being thrown in the bin along with hundreds of others by the first scrutineer, who would be the Superintendent for England North East, a vast area stretching from the Nottinghamshire border to the Scottish one. He was ex-military; I obviously wasn't, apart from my forgettable few months in the navy, but I did already work for the RSPCA, albeit in the lowliest capacity and with an invisible driving licence, and I had actually met the chap when he came to see us at the Hull rescue centre.

If I got past that one, I felt I had another advantage: Carol. We were married by this time and RSPCA inspectors' wives are an important part of the set-up, as unpaid personal assistants. I knew that if the superintendent met her, that would be a gold star on my form. And so it proved. Next, I was asked to appear before the selection board at HQ, Horsham, and a formidable experience that was – like a rabbit being interviewed by England's most senior foxes.

Somehow I got through that, and so on to the very concentrated six-month training course, varying from the academic – you have to know the law inside out as it relates to animals –to the extremely practical, such as abseiling down a cliff to rescue a cat, and spending a week working in a slaughterhouse. Not even the abattoir was going to stop me, now I was on my way to my perfect job.

If you divided that job of RSPCA Inspector: Scorswick, in the standard way – into objectives, responsibilities and circumstances – I couldn't see how it could be bettered. The circumstances included a salary that wouldn't make many people groan with envy but was adequate. I was supplied with a new Ford Escort van fully equipped, uniform, and a house within a modest price limit. My piece of God's own broad acres was mostly rural but there were towns.

Also, the RSPCA relief system meant that I had alternate weekends off but, during the weekends on, I covered for one of my neighbour inspectors across his territory, thus doubling my workload. At one time or another I could count pretty well all the great features of the Yorkshire-scape, from coast to moors to dales and back again. It was decidedly the green and pleasant land. I loved the rolling countryside, I loved the ducks on the pond, and I loved the classic English villages, the mix of cottages, some finer houses, pub, church, shop, school, a delight to the eye and the heart.

RSPCA inspectors were given a six-monthly checking over by their regional superintendent, and mine was a big, blunt Yorkshireman of the Jack Hartley type, called Fred Sheriff. He was a natural for his job, keen of eye and brain, mighty of aspect, impatient of footlers and fiddlers, thoroughly experienced and completely trustworthy. Management sometimes seems to attract politicians, ladder climbers who use other people as rungs. Fred wasn't like that. He was there because he was there. No politician would ever shift him.

He wanted to see that I understood my responsibilities, that all my paperwork was in order, my house was in order and my orders were in order. He also wanted to know that my family was happy, my children were fit and healthy, and most of all that he would be able to have a second and third slice with his tea of Carol's special chocolate cake, RSPCA superintendents for the pleasuring of. This magnificent structure of three layers of chocolate ambrosia, touched by angels with whipped cream in between, always ensured that, on the very rare occasions that there was any wintry discontent, it was made glorious summer for all the sons of York present at the time.

On his first visit, of course he didn't know about the chocolate cake and so he piled in. Had I introduced myself to the police, the fire service, the social services, the local vets? Were my firearms in perfect condition? We were issued with a .32 pistol – a World War Two vintage repeater, modified from nine shots to two and mainly for putting down horses – and a captive ball pistol as humane killer for other, large animals.

Was my drugs register up to the minute and did it match exactly with my stock? We had to euthanise animals sometimes, mostly alone and never with the help of a veterinary nurse, and so our reports, being the only evidence, had to be meticulous. When he saw that I was a disciplined and conscientious keeper of records and kit, he eased off and we became good friends. He was only making sure, after all, that I was doing my job properly and, since I thought it the ideal job in Utopia, that didn't represent a difficulty.

The other big issue the superintendents looked out for was your partner in life. The RSPCA didn't pay Carol anything but she was crucial to the job. We were in Yellow Pages. In my area, it wasn't just me that was the RSPCA. It was both of us. Carol had to take messages, make judgements on their priority, get in touch with me somehow in the age before mobile phones, keep angry people at a suitable distance and distressed people calm. She was very good at it.

The final part of the job spec is objectives, and that can be summed up very easily: solve every problem that has anything at all to do with animals. It could be a cow stuck halfway down a ravine, a goose wandering around a pub car park or a tortoise trying to cross the road. It could be an accusation of cruelty or, worse in some ways, a rumour of cruelty. It could be a cat up a tree, a fugitive anaconda, an escaped budgerigar, a goat in someone's garden eating the strawberries or someone who insisted on keeping five goats and a horse in the dining room.

There were wildlife criminals like badger diggers, birds' eggers, bird trappers and bird-of-prey poisoners. There were wildlife UFO spotters who that very minute had seen the Phantom Black Panther of Cleckuddersfax, and there was everything in between.

I was on 24-hour call all the time, except on those alternate weekends when my telephone was diverted to a neighbouring inspector. The other weekend brought us the double calls. There was an official RSPCA brass plaque outside the house. The word soon spread through the village and surrounding districts and I grew to become a local figure, like the doctor or the dentist, the village postmistress, the vicar, the vet or the undertaker, and from time to time I had to be bits of all of those.

We had a switch on the telephone that allowed calls through only to our private number when I was off duty. It diverted calls made to the RSPCA number. This was fine, except that the police and all sorts of other people knew where we lived. If they couldn't get through on the phone, they'd knock on our door and present us with a litter of kittens, an injured owl, a myxy rabbit, any kind of stray – foxes, badgers, young otters, hedgehogs. Some folk were genuinely concerned, some were over-concerned, and some saw us as a convenient way to get rid of an inconvenient animal.

I really never knew what was going to happen next, except with people like Mrs Stokesley. Every RSPCA inspector acquires regular customers. These may be animal lovers, misguided perhaps, or over-optimistic about what they can take on. Or they may be in the business, making a living or extra cash from animals, careless about welfare or downright cynical about it. If the latter, they may become regular customers of the magistrates too.

Mrs Stokesley lived with her daughter in a big old terraced house on one of the main residential streets in Scorswick. Her neighbours likewise had big old terraced houses but the difference was that they were normal families, seemingly with sufficient income to maintain a pleasant lifestyle. Mrs Stokesley's family, daughter apart, consisted entirely of stray dogs, and she clearly didn't have the money to cope. Even so, she could not resist taking in a dog, any dog, and I think that some people who were fed up with looking after a dog, or surprised that a Christmas puppy actually needed any looking after, would offload the animal onto Mrs Stokesley rather than have the embarrassment of taking it to the RSPCA or the vet.

I'd often be round there, following a complaint or because I was passing, and I'd find a dog with distemper or demodectic mange. This is caused by a mite of the demodex family which lives in the follicles of all sorts of animals, including humans, mostly doing no harm at all. In certain circumstances, such as when a dog has a weakened immune system, the mites go mad, cause dreadful itching, which makes the dog go crackers trying to scratch and bite itself, producing wounds that become infected. Result: dog covered in pus and bloody sores, suffering terribly.

Sometimes Mrs Stokesley would not resist my taking a dog away entirely; sometimes I would have to have it treated but bring it back. I wouldn't say we had a relationship of sunshine and light but we did get on reasonably well. We were both trying to do the right thing in our different ways.

For one reason or another I hadn't been to see Mrs Stokesley for a few months and things had got out of hand. The neighbours were complaining loudly about the smell. One said there was liquid dog sewage seeping through her walls where the floor joists met. The council had served numerous notices on Mrs Stokesley, telling her she must reduce the number of dogs and keep to certain standards, but she ignored them.

A court order was obtained, with the right to use force to gain entry, and I had phone calls from the council and the police summoning me to the occasion. I was not looking forward to this job at all. Not only would I be in my accustomed role, protecting the thin blue line from a canine savaging, but I knew Mrs Stokesley. She would be very upset and she'd blame me, and I'd be the one to go in first.

Sure enough, when I arrived there were police and council officers waiting. I was acquainted with them all by now, and they were very happy to give me a cheery welcome and swap some friendly banter, while stepping well out of the way. Mrs Stokesley had been warned, by the established technique of shouting through the letterbox, that she was not to obstruct the officers in the course of their duty or she would be arrested.

So, when I rang the bell and Mrs Stokesley came to the door, I was The Officers. I was the embodiment of the law and of the forces of evil. Despite the semi-circle of council people and grinning constables behind me, I was it.

Mrs and Miss Stokesley stood aside to let me in, their eyes emitting a stream of invisible poisoned darts. While they were proving beyond doubt that thought transference is possible, I was also struck by wave after wave of the most appalling, nauseating stench. In the sitting room and kitchen, both bare of furniture, was a collection of a dozen dogs or more, all sorts, some identifiable breeds like Alsatian and basset hound, two lurchers, some mongrel terriers, some Labrador types, some barking at me, some looking hopeful and wagging their tails, all trying to make the best of it in an ocean of dog mess.

I'd say the average depth of this especially potent quickmud was seven or eight inches. It certainly made me wish I'd put my wellies on as I slipped and slid around, trying to round up these dogs, wishing the RSPCA issued their inspectors with gas masks. Most of the animals were in reasonable shape. Some were showing early signs of mange, some were a little underweight but nothing too serious. What was serious was the constant flow of invective from the women. They'd geared up from silent hatred to all-out verbal warfare. No swear word or combination of swear words, no fatal curse nor hellish imprecation was left to idle in obscurity as they followed me to and from the door.

There was no room in my van for all of the dogs. I could only take them three or four at a time. Since the police refused to go near and the council people likewise, my only option was to do just that, ferry them in batches to the temporary home I'd lined up at the local boarding kennels. There they would be washed and fed and kept in decent surroundings for a day or two until I could get them to York.

The round trip took me about half an hour. Each time I returned, the crowd outside the house had increased in size. It was a cold day but that didn't deter anyone. Kids on bikes sucked sweets and pointed at the funny man in the hat with dog muck all over him. Police officers explained the situation to little old ladies passing by. Council officials poured themselves coffee from their flasks.

As I waded, literally, through my task, the cursing from Mrs and Miss Stokesley got worse and worse. I was a bit miffed at this. I didn't deserve it. I was only trying to help the dogs they had been trying to help. Anyway, I dealt with a big white Alsatian and I was down to my last dog, a mixture of small terrier breeds with maybe a touch of border collie. It had been standing against the kitchen door when I last saw it but when I came to fetch it, it was wedged behind the gas cooker.

There were no tables or chairs in the kitchen, just this cooker, and a sink unit and a couple of cupboards that looked like utility stuff from soon after the war. On the cooker was a pan of water, boiling. I very briefly entertained the notion that Mrs Stokesley had changed personalities and was going to offer us all tea and buns, but I couldn't see any cups or anywhere to stand any cups. Maybe she was about to boil an egg.

I bent down to retrieve the little dog from its uncomfortable spot, wondering quite how it had managed to get in there. The daughter shouted something. It sounded like 'Go on, Mum, now, get the ****ing ****,' or words to that effect. Almost at the same instant I felt a searing pain down the side of my face and I heard dear mum say, 'Have that, you bastard.' I'm not sure what I said, or if I said anything beyond a screaming yell, but I put my hand to where the agony was and took it away again. I looked in horror at what was in my hand. As well as the muck and hairs from picking up filthy dogs, there was a tangled pile of shreds that looked awfully like skin. My skin.

With a bang and a rattle, Mrs Stokesley dropped the pan on the floor. Well, at least she wasn't going to whack me with it. I hurried outside with the dog, which fortunately hadn't taken any of the carefully aimed boiling water, with Mrs Stokesley in hot pursuit telling me she was very sorry – very sorry, that is, that it hadn't been a full barrel of boiling oil. Sergeant Wainwright, the same old-fashioned copper who had rung me from the station about dead Alf, sprang into action, arresting Mrs Stokesley and daughter and telling the WPC I knew from the Siege of Alf's Fleas, to get me to the hospital. I put the terrier in my van and jumped into the police car for my blue-light, white-knuckle ride to Scorswick hospital, where they took me in on the instant, stripped me and washed me, and began smearing me with slimy substances.

WPC Bluelight hared off to pick up Carol but wouldn't tell her what had happened, presumably because of police procedure, so when my dear wife arrived she was expecting to find me at death's door or possibly already over the threshold. As she was eight months' pregnant with our first, there were other possibilities too, so I'm sure her tears were of relief when she found me only parboiled, with fifteen-sixteenths of my surface area still recognisable.

The doctors wanted me in for two days. I thought one night would be sufficient. Carol pointed out that if I went back to work with my face looking like it did, as if I'd been starring in *The Wicker Man* but somehow managed to escape halfway through the ceremony, I could be the cause of a sharp rise in the incidence of doorstep heart attacks. This discussion went on for a while and none of us paid much attention to Sergeant Wainwright slipping silently into the room, apologetically, as he might if arriving late for his daughter's performance in the school nativity play. At an opportune moment, he gave a cough, likewise apologetic.

'Er, if I may have your attention,' he began, and we all gave him it. 'It's the van. The RSPCA van. It's causing an obstruction.' The members of the assembly looked at each other. The good sergeant, divining that the message in the air said, 'So why don't you move it?', gave us his reason.

'One of the dogs in the van is an Alsatian, a particularly large Alsatian, and it rather seems to have decided that it has a duty to the van, to, er, protect it.' He stopped short of asking me directly to leave my deathbed for a short time in order to effect removal of said obstacle, but the implication was clear.

'Huh harjun ih kwy rye,' I said, speaking through hard-boiled lips. 'Ih a bih wye woh.'

Carol, at first unable to believe what she'd been hearing, let rip. She would never use any of the words I'd heard earlier from Mrs Stokesley and her oratory was all the more powerful for that. Could the sergeant not see that her precious husband (me) had been lobsterised? Why couldn't he, a substantial and healthy police officer, doubtless with a clean driving licence, move the such-and-such, so-and-so of a van his such-and-such, so-and-so self? What was the matter with the peacekeepers of Scorswick? Couldn't they reach the pedals with their big flat feet?

While Sergeant Wainwright reeled back under the onslaught, I tried to explain to Carol about this chink in the otherwise sturdy, reliable and fearless wall that was our police force. Even animal lovers like Sergeant Wainwright would never go near a locked-up dog, and this was an Alsatian. A big white one. Carol would not be mollified.

'Alsatians are what the police have,' she cried, incredulously. 'Police dogs are Alsatians. That PC on Z Cars has an Alsatian. What are you talking about?'

Well, if our fantastic police force wouldn't shift the van, she, Carol, a feeble and frail member of the weaker sex, moreover great with child, would do it for them.

'Have you got a copy of the *Daily Mirror* anywhere?' she asked a nurse. 'The tabloids are better to roll up than the broadsheets. For tapping badly behaved dogs on the nose. They're better for that.'

Sergeant Wainwright harrumphed something about

not being able to allow, in the circumstances, RSPCA vehicle, possibly insurance not covering, risk of dog bite, member of the public. Carol, deeply and mightily annoyed at being labelled a member of the public, was again speechless. If there was a moment when she might have gone into premature labour, this was it, and if there had been a surgeon's scalpel to hand, I feel sure she would have offered to slit the sergeant's throat with it. I took the opportunity to slide out of bed, put on my hospital slippers, and accompany him to his car.

All this was a little out of character for my friend Doug Wainwright, not normally one to bother greatly about proper procedure. He was indeed a substantial fellow, well over six feet and a big physical presence in any company. He wouldn't have needed gloves to be a wicket keeper; his hands were massive. Nowadays he'd be called unreconstructed; he would say that the only thing the initials PC stood for was police constable. Like many of the old-fashioned sort, seemingly bluff, brusque and hard, he had his soft spot, and his particular weakness happened to be animals in trouble, which suited me very well.

Anyway, after my boiling, here was the sarge giving me another blue-light whizz through the streets of Scorswick, after which I had a quiet word with the white Alsatian, drove my van to the kennels where the other dogs were, unloaded, and allowed myself to be returned to my hospital bed.

One of things I liked about my job was the complete responsibility. My area and everything in it was down to me, but the other side of that is having no one to turn to when you're taking time off. The neighbouring inspectors do their best with your diverted calls, as you do with theirs, but we always have our own work full to capacity. Inevitably, the calls pile high. Lying in bed in hospital, I knew this was happening, and it wasn't only like an in-tray rising: every call represented some form of distress being suffered by an animal. Every delay possibly increased the distress.

It wasn't long, about twenty-four hours, before the in-tray defeated the doctors, the nurses, even Carol, and I was out on the streets, knocking on doors and frightening people with my face tartare. Meanwhile Mrs and Miss Stokesley were released on bail. Mrs had been charged with aggravated assault, Miss with aiding and abetting. With no dogs to distract them, maybe they would give their house a bit of a clean.

Six months later they pleaded not guilty at the Crown Court. I'd had plenty of experience giving evidence to magistrates but this was my first time before the intimidating formality of a judge and jury. Not that Mrs Stokesley was intimidated. She said I'd knocked the pan of boiling water onto my head by accident. In which case, said I when it was my turn, why did she shout 'Have that, you bastard', and why did she say something very similar to the council public-health chap when she threw my dog-grasper at him? There were pictures of this last incident too, taken by the local press photographer.

The trial took four days; the jury took about as many minutes to find the two women guilty. The judge handed down a suspended prison sentence and a community service order, and that was the end of our beautiful friendship. Of course it hit the papers. RSPCA in Hot Water. Woman Boils Man. Dog Woman Turns Poacher. The nationals picked it up and, as they do, gave me plenty of false quotations. 'I can't even bear to fill the kettle,' said Inspector Langdale. 'And it's fried eggs only from now on.'

If it happened today I'd be offered counselling and I could probably sue somebody for giving me an emotionally crippling aversion to hot showers. All I got then was a lot of slather in the pub and, oh dear, a phone call from HQ.

Calls from headquarters were rarer than cries for help from maltreated brontosauruses, and this wasn't any old HQ busybody wanting to know why I needed a new windscreen wiper. It was our legal superintendent, the guy who went through our case files and who was our point of reference on all matters to do with the law. He was a man of quiet authority and considerable knowledge, greatly respected by all, and he was very disappointed in me.

'Why is it,' he wanted to know, 'that I've had to learn about your boiling water assault from the *Daily Express*? Are you such a brilliant solo operator, Inspector Langdale, the very James Bond of the RSPCA, that you are licensed to do whatever you like without reference to anyone? Or perhaps you are so thick that you can't see a connection between an assault while at work, a court case, and the RSPCA legal department?'

'No, no,' I said. 'It's just me being . . . sorry, I mean . . . been so busy lately, I find I've not had . . .' That was an error of judgement.

'Oh, I see,' said the legal eagle. 'I see. Well, what *I* find is that all the other inspectors of my acquaintance seem able to find time in their busy days to follow basic procedure. I find that they find time for it.'

'Ah, um,' was all I could manage, or something of the sort.

'Possibly, just possibly,' he went on, 'the job is too much for you. Too many things happening at once. Things fall apart, the centre cannot hold. You should consider something a little less fraught. Have a look in the *Yorkshire Post*. Do they want a lighthouse keeper on Flamborough Head? Do we have enough lollipop ladies in Scorswick?'

There was nothing I could do but apologise and promise that it would never happen again. That was my first HQ rollicking and, in all my years with the RSPCA I only ever had one other. Unfortunately for my reputation among those who dwell in marble halls, it came very soon after the first one.

5

SEE YOU LATER, ALLIGATOR

'What on earth is that?' said Carol, as I opened the van doors. The object of her curiosity was a large metal box about a yard square, painted green, with various knobs, switches and dials set into one side of it.

'I got it very cheap,' I said. 'Army surplus. This will save us a load of time and effort. I'm collecting the aerial later.'

'Aerial? We already have an aerial. For the television. It gets BBC2 and Channel Four, BBC1 and ITV, and there aren't any more stations. So we don't need an aerial.'

'Ah no, you see, this is not so much an aerial, in fact. More of a sort of a mast. It has to be quite high or we won't get the distance.'

'Distance? How high is quite high?' Carol enquired.

And so it was that we became the operators of Radio Langdale, with an eighteen-foot mast on our bungalow roof, a transmitter/receiver the size of an old radiogram in our sitting room, and the ability to communicate at any time and, regardless of the positioning of telephone boxes, anywhere in a thirty-mile radius. This was a blessing that those of the smartphone generation may not understand – and they probably haven't seen those black and white war films either. To the sound of machine guns, the wireless operator sits in front of the big box under a camouflage net, adjusting dials but getting nothing in his headphones as the crump of artillery fire sounds, not too far away. 'Sorry, sir. Can't raise them.' 'Keep trying, corporal.'

When the first mobile phones came out, our local manager at British Telecom asked me to take one on trial. I gave it him back after a while. I'd rather have my radio, I said. That thing's so big and heavy, I'm risking pulling a muscle every time I lift it to my ear.

My old routine had been to call in to Carol on a public telephone every so often to pick up messages. Sod's Law dictated that should I have spent the last hour or two driving north, the message would be about an urgent matter in the far south. Now, Carol could contact me as soon as anything happened.

If there'd been nothing urgent that morning, I would call in on Radio Langdale when I stopped to eat my sandwiches. Carol agreed to this provided that no message from her could be so important that sandwich finishing was prevented. Knowing what stress such a regulation could cause, I made a point of finishing the cheese and tomato or Shippam's shrimp paste before calling her, so that I only had a Waggon Wheel or a Penguin to manage as I drove off to whatever crisis Carol had told me about.

One that didn't sound much like a crisis but would very shortly turn that way, was The Case of the Overgrown Alligator. A pet-shop owner I knew well had rung in to say that one of his friends, who had kept an alligator for twenty years, all legal and licensed, was beginning to feel that this wasn't perhaps the ideal pet after all. The animal, called Samson, had been one of two brought into the country from Florida as youthful livewires about eight inches long. The other had died but Samson had responded well to his new owner's care and attention, growing into bigger and bigger vivaria until there was no vivarium to be had that was big enough.

That was the time when the owner should have taken the steps he was now taking. He should have found somewhere to rehouse Samson. However, that's all very well to say but the chap was fond of Samson and, not having a wife or live-in beloved with whom to discuss the matter – perhaps one who might have made suggestions along the lines of 'It's me or that alligator'– he could see no other choice but to convert his bathroom into a reptile house.

The conventional fittings were removed and, with extra strength tiling all around, a raised pool was constructed about six feet by six, and eighteen inches deep. Proper heaters and ultra-violet lights completed a comfortable if restricted home for Samson and, again, things were fine for a while.

The beast kept on growing. At the point where I entered the story, Samson was about seven feet long. His owner could not manage him at all. The only contact was at feeding time when the bathroom door was opened a few inches, chicken legs were rapidly hurled in and the door slammed shut before Samson, jaws agape and legs paddling, could make the reacquaintance with his keeper that he so obviously desired.

The pet-shop owner, as intermediary, a friend in need, asked me if the situation could be handled discreetly. The chap had this alligator legally and he didn't want a fuss with the neighbours or the newspapers. He just wanted Samson to be rehomed 'somewhere nice'.

I arranged to call round at the house, a smart detached on a leafy residential street in Scorswick, and there met Andy, the owner, a pleasant fellow who was well informed on alligators and was clearly most upset about the mess he'd got Samson into. He felt guilty about leaving things so long and was desperately worried that Samson would have to be put down, but had every confidence that I could find the answer and, of course, somewhere nice.

'The RSPCA will never let you down,' I said. 'Now, I'd better have a look at Samson.'

'Is that really necessary?' said Andy. 'I've already fed

him, you see.' I told him I did need to see what I was up against. Anyway, I'd never been close to a big 'gator before, not at that stage of my career anyway. He went through the back of the house to the freezer and returned with two chicken legs.

'Can I feed him one?' I asked.

'Oh no, no, not really. Er, there's a knack to it.'

We went up the stairs. He had me stand a little to the left and away from the bathroom door, so that I could see in when it was opened.

'Don't blink or you'll miss it,' he said. I nodded, beginning to feel nervous. Andy was tense, and his tenseness was infectious. He glanced at me to see if I was ready. I swallowed and nodded. He turned the handle, opened the door no more than six inches, threw in the chicken pieces and banged the door shut again, at the same moment as it was almost blown off its hinges by the impact of a seemingly airborne seven-foot alligator.

I'd had enough time to see gaping jaws, huge teeth and malevolent eyes, and when Andy turned to me with his back against the bathroom door, I found I was pressing my own back into the wall, realising I had not made any kind of a plan about which way to run should Samson have destroyed his temple.

It could not be doubted that Andy had a problem requiring an urgent solution. One day soon, he and the bathroom door could turn into a launching platform for an escaped and hungry alligator. The police would have to shoot Samson, and what might happen before they got to him didn't bear thinking about.

I promised I'd get on to it and spent the next few days phoning every zoo and animal collection in the UK. London, Whipsnade, Chester, Flamingo Land, Edinburgh, all of them. They already had alligators and didn't want another, but I was given a lead to a Dutchman called Wim, living in southern Spain, who had an exotic wildlife collection. I was on to him straightaway but at first he didn't seem too keen, mainly because of the logistics implied in transferring such an animal privately – I was to be transport manager – across Europe. I pointed out that the alternative was a bullet in the head or an overdose of barbiturate in a back leg. He was my only hope, and he eventually agreed that he would take Samson if I could get him there.

I got quite excited about this. The climate in southern Spain would mean Samson could spend most of his time out in the open, and Wim had other alligators. Maybe one would be the alligator equivalent of Delilah. I recalled the film from my boyhood. Maybe in Samson's eyes there would be a 'gator as lovely as Hedy Lamarr, while he strutted his Victor Mature muscles poolside, in the Spanish sunshine.

It's amazing what you can do if you try, and I went right to the top to find a way of transporting Samson. British Airways agreed to take him for nothing, to the nearest Spanish airport. I was thrilled to bits, problem solved, until I was warned by an expert on Crocodilia that the stress of air travel might prove fatal. I couldn't see it myself. Samson was not your typical wild-caught alligator, shocked by being put in a foreign crate. He'd lived in a confined space for twenty years. He was seven feet long and three feet wide and as fit as could be, but I had been warned.

Publicity is always the bait in operations like this. Wim wanted some for his reptile park and BA wanted some for their charitable work, so I turned to the good old BBC who were delighted at the prospect of a story featuring a dangerous wild animal in suburbia.

British Airways insisted that a paying passenger should accompany Samson, not unreasonably, in case of any trouble. There would be no question of the RSPCA paying for me to go on the flight. I didn't even bother asking. I phoned Wim, obviously a fairly wealthy man, and got him to come over, ready to act as courier and nurse. Now, all we had to do was put Samson in his travelling case.

Then my boss intervened. Fred Sheriff had been on holiday at the crucial moments when the arrangements all fell into place, and somehow I had neglected to inform him before, when (I said to myself) there was nothing to tell because it wasn't fixed up yet. Anyway, my proud little message about rehoming Samson was on Fred's desk when he came back to work, and my ear was welding itself to the telephone a few minutes later.

'Now then, Carter, what's all this about an alligator?'

'Hello, Fred. You got my message. Yes, well, it's got to be rehomed. I mean, the man's got it in his bathroom.'

'This is way outside your responsibilities, Inspector Langdale.' Oh dear. That was a bad sign, not calling me Carter. 'Rehoming alligators, lions, tigers and camels is not your job. You know what your job is, and if you want to keep it you had better stick to it.'

I tried to ask him whose job it was, if it wasn't mine, but that only turned up the roasting temperature. I harboured unworthy thoughts. Next time he came to our house for tea it wouldn't be Carol's chocolate cake. It would be beetroot sandwiches and a Carr's water biscuit.

I reviewed the situation. In the blue corner were British Airways, disappointed that a neat little PR coup could not be pulled off; Wim, who had now become really enthusiastic about the whole thing; Andy, who still had his alligator; the BBC, fed up that a memorable news story would not now be made; me, totally frustrated and, although he didn't know it, Samson, due to exchange a new life of sun, sand and lady alligators for oblivion. In the red corner was Fred, the judge who had given his verdict.

If I couldn't do it as an RSPCA man, I would do it as a private individual. I got a hire firm to lend me a Ford Transit free. A local joiner agreed to make the crate for nothing, big enough but with no extra room for Samson to thrash about and injure himself. I got P&O to give me a free ride across the Channel. I'd have to pay for the petrol but I persuaded Dan, an RSPCA colleague and old pal, to agree to share the driving with Wim and me. We would take Samson there and drive back over a weekend. I phoned the BBC. We were on again, next Saturday morning.

The first phase of our not entirely cunning plan was to have Andy turn off the heat in Samson's pool on the Friday night. Reptiles thermo-regulate, that is, they are only active when the ambient temperature is suitably warm. If Samson was cooler than usual, he would be lethargic, slow, and easier to deal with.

The TV crew assembled, cracking unnecessary jokes. Wim stood ready, armed with a towel and some gaffer tape. Dan and I stood ready, not armed with anything.

'It's all right,' said Wim. 'I'll get the towel over his head, then he won't be able to see. If he can't see, he'll be still, like a chicken in a sack.' Some chicken, I thought, and where's the sack? 'Don't worry, my friends. I have done this before. All I need is enough time to get the tape around his jaws.' I could see Dan was wondering the same as me. How much time is enough?

Andy, relegated to concerned spectator, looked on like a boxer's mother, wanting her boy to win but without anyone getting hurt. We opened the bathroom door. Samson looked up but didn't move. Three hearty cheers for thermo-regulation, we thought, as Wim began the countdown.

'Three. Two. One. Go!' and he jumped on Samson's

head with his towel, gaffer tape in hand. As a mere safety precaution, with no danger whatsoever to ourselves, Dan and I jumped fractionally after Wim, me heading for the midriff while Dan sat on the tail, slamming the door shut behind us, and we immediately discovered several things about alligators. One was that 'cooler than usual' counted for nothing. We now knew that whatever regulations apply in freestyle bathroom alligator wrestling, thermo is not one of them. Two was that alligators are very powerful.

Wim, loudly deploying a vehement mixture of Dutch and Anglo-Saxon, made it plain, as if we needed telling, that if anyone let go, we'd had it. Dan and I, feeling the full strength of a very angry Samson devoted entirely to the instant demise of his tormentors, were at the limits of our physical abilities. It needed all three of us to subdue Samson and, at several points in the procedure, three didn't seem as many as we'd have liked. The camera crew, outside the door and unable to see in, were enjoying listening to the sound effects, quite unaware of what would happen if any of us three lost his grip.

After what can truly be termed a titanic struggle, we got Samson into defeat mode and carried him out. Cameras rolled, Andy burst into tears, and we screwed the lid down on Samson with utter relief. Dan and I looked at each other, sweating, shaking, breathing like pearl divers, hoping the other one looked as bad. Wim tried to seem calm, grinning inanely at the TV people, like he wrestled alligators before breakfast each morning except Sunday, and couldn't understand why everybody else didn't follow the same low-key exercise regime.

It was the work of a moment to slide Samson's box into the back of the Transit, and off we headed for the motorway. Once we were down the sliproad and cruising along, the miles flying by, we thought we'd cracked it. Then, there was a banging and crashing from behind us. Looking through the little window in the back of the cab, I could see the nose-end of an alligator jaw sticking up, as if sniffing the air. In retrospect, an escaping alligator probably would have scored enough marks to classify as an emergency and we could have pulled on to the hard shoulder. In our heightened state of adrenalin-fuelled awareness, or panic, all we could think of doing was aiming for the next junction as fast as possible. Dan put his foot down while Wim and I watched Samson's snout. Occasionally he seemed to give up and retreat into the box. Then there'd be a renewed assault and a further inch of snout would be revealed.

Off at the junction, park at the nearest available spot, leap out, open van doors, feel eternally grateful that Samson was in retreat at that moment, bang in extra nails and more screws until we were quite sure that neither Samson nor Houdini could get out – a predictable scene, made more colourful by the large saloon car pulling up behind us, gaily done out in a fetching combination of white, red and orange stripes.

The motor-patrol police sergeant, in shirtsleeves and sunglasses, put on and adjusted his hat as he strolled towards us. The other officer was on the radio, presumably checking on the last whereabouts of a blue Ford Transit, reg foxtrot juliet wotsit, probably stolen. I reached for my RSPCA identity card and saw the sergeant stiffen.

'It's okay,' I said. 'RSPCA. We've got an alligator.' He looked at my ID without comment, and peered inside the van. Wim and Dan were still in there, with hammer and screwdriver.

'He's called Samson,' I said, making conversation. 'He was trying to get out of his box, so we thought we'd better run for it and bang him up quick.' The other policeman joined us.

'It's a hire van, Sarge,' he said. 'I asked them to check. It's for taking an alligator to Spain.'

The sergeant, still without a word, lifted his hat, scratched his head with the same hand, pulled the hat firmly on again, and set off back to his car. We stood and watched as they drove away.

There were no further incidents on our drive to Dover, where we joined the queue for the ferry. There was an unusual amount of customs activity, with maybe half or more of the vehicles being inspected, but we were waved through. On our ticket it said something like 'Nature of load' and beside that was written 'Alligator'.

In France it soon became clear that Dan and I were going to have to do all the driving. Wim could not get on with a steering wheel on the wrong side of the dashboard, which meant that turns would have to be taken trying to get some proper kip, and the only place to do that was in the back of the van beside Samson. Dan went first. I drove.

'Wim,' I said. 'Keep an eye on him, will you? I know Dan. He's a heavy sleeper.' Wim rummaged in his bag and took out a neat little camera and, through the window behind us, took a photograph.

'I think,' he said, 'that if Samson gets out, Mrs Dan will want to know that her husband was eaten in action.'

The TV crew had flown out with Andy, to be there to film us arriving and unloading, and it was a magnificent sight. Samson slid out of his box and into his own private pool, about ten feet square and four feet deep, and after a quarter of an hour enjoying that, he climbed out onto one of his selection of basking areas and settled down to absorb a few rays.

To the manner born, we thought, with the most gratifying sense of satisfaction. We all shook hands. Andy had tears in his eyes again and even hardened old pros like Dan and me had to admit to a bit of a sniffle.

We only had time for a quick look around Wim's place, which was croc heaven for just about every species of the family, and a meal, before were back on the road, driving and sleeping, sleeping and driving, to be home in time for work on the Monday morning.

I'd already alerted my contacts on the local rag, and

they ran the story which was picked up by three of the nationals as well as the *Yorkshire Post*. It was on Yorkshire TV news too, and the BBC gave it the full treatment, so everyone who had helped us got some good PR out of it.

Fred rang. He was not happy. I'd gone directly against his instructions. I said I'd done it in my own time, at my own expense, so it wasn't an RSPCA matter. Oh yes it was, and he was going to think about it, and consider the pros and cons, and very likely find a ton of bricks which he could use as a model for his future actions regarding himself and me, gravity-wise.

Oh, that's all right then, I thought. Good old Fred. Without a care I got on with my normal work until, a week or two later, Carol took a message. Fred had been seconded on a sabbatical, or something, and his stand-in seemed to be a completely different kettle of fish. He was going to come and see me, and give me an official interview with a view to disciplinary measures.

I was shocked and hurt by this, and couldn't understand. If I hadn't loved my job so much I'd have told them where they could put their disciplinary measures. I talked it over with Carol and we came up with a plan.

The man arrived and he did look like a fish but not the sort you put in a kettle, more one of those that live in darkness at unfathomable depths and lead their prey towards their huge needle teeth with a kindly light. We sat across from each other at the dining table. He shuffled his papers and pretended to read. I was supposed to wait in trembling fear until he deigned to speak.

'I don't know if you have it there,' I said, brightly, 'but we got a lot of good publicity from Samson. Lots of excellent stuff, in the papers, on the radio and the telly.' No response. 'Yes,' I continued, 'the RSPCA did very well out of it. Everybody singing our praises. I bet the old collecting tins were rattling fifty to the dozen.' Still no response. I took a deep breath. 'What a shame it would be,' I said, all innocent, 'if I had to go back to those same media people and tell them I was going to be disciplined over it.'

The deep-sea fish crumpled up his papers, straightened them out again, put his files neatly back in his briefcase, rose, and said that senior management had decided to overlook my extraordinary behaviour this time. As he headed down the path to his car, Carol put the kettle on and cut a couple of slices of chocolate cake.

Still, the story wasn't finished. The phone rang. It was Wim. How were we all, did we get home okay, yes we did, we were fine, how was Samson? 'This is it,' said Wim. 'I had him checked over by the vet, and I've had to give him a new name. I thought about Delilah but decided on Salome instead.'

6

HAPPY CHRISTMAS, YOUR LORDSHIP

It was shortly before Christmas and I was about to set out for York and our annual RSPCA staff dinner. These were brilliant events and I was really looking forward to it. All our calls would be fielded by the neighbouring RSPCA region, as we'd already done for them, and we could have a stress-free evening.

One of our office girls phoned me. There was this problem, it was on my way, I could look in, it wouldn't take a minute, it's just that the man was very insistent, and he did own half the county. She filled me in on the details.

Viscount X had been out two days before watching a shoot and had taken his ladyship's West Highland White terrier with him for the walk. Wanting to see something particular, he'd stuck his walking stick in the ground, fastened the terrier to it and gone off for a few minutes. When he came back the terrier had vanished and my lord realised he'd parked the animal right next to a badger sett. His staff had conducted a complete search of the estate and endured two nights' vigil by the sett, with no result.

Westies are popular these days as pets and, because of their looks, they might be thought of as jolly little lapdogs, forgetting what they were bred for. They, like their relatives the Cairn and Skye terriers and the famous Scottie, are of an ancient race, built for work in the hard terrain and sometimes very rough weather of the Highlands. They have strong legs ideal for digging, and their sworn foes are the rat, the fox and the badger, which live down holes.

My lord's Westie had done nothing more than return to its ancestral duties, and its instincts had taken it far into enemy territory. As I arrived, Plan B was about to be implemented, which I found shocking enough, but not as shocking as recognising a certain aristocratic chap whose Rolls-Royce I had shunted when covered in fleas. Luckily, he didn't recognise me in full uniform and I hoped things would stay that way.

'Ah, Inspector, thank goodness you're here,' said the viscount. 'You can advise this fellow where to start.'

'This fellow, my lord?'

'Yes, he's going to drive the JCB thing.'

'I'm sorry, my lord, but I can't let you dig up a badger sett with a JCB. It's against the law.'

'What's that got to do with it? I'm chairman of the bench.'

'I don't care if you're the Archangel Gabriel, you're not digging up a badger sett.'

This was a fellow unused to being contradicted and he was quite taken aback. Obviously I had not understood the gravity of the situation so, grasping my arm, he led me aside to explain the horror of it all, man to man.

'Look here, Inspector,' he said – or words to that effect. 'It's my wife's dog, and my fault. It's surely gone down the sett. My wife and daughters have made it plain to me that Christmas will not occur this year, nor possibly any other year, if I do not retrieve that which I have lost. The entire festive season and very probably the rest of my life will be spent in isolation. Dinner will be cold shoulder and hot tongue. You see?'

A parade followed, his lordship striding out in the lead, me following with my low-tech situation-retrieving kit, being a bundle of slim iron rods, a rubber mallet and a stethoscope, and a dozen miscellaneous estate workers in line astern. When we reached the sett I could see a big problem. The sett, going by the size of it, was an ancestral home for a family going back even further than his lordship's.

The stethoscope is an instrument that always inspires respect, and there was deep silence around me as I began my methodical exploration, thrusting a rod into the soil and placing my stethoscope on it to listen for vibrations. Nothing there, so we'll try here, and here. There was no need to ask for quiet. The deference shown to the expert stethoscoper could not have been greater had I been a druid weaving a spell before true believers. In fact, it was a technique we law-abiders learned from badger diggers, who search setts for tunnelling activity in this way.

As I progressed, I needed my mallet to drive a rod into some stony ground and, since it was more or less at his feet, I asked his lordship if he'd pass it to me.

'Perkins,' said he to a man twenty yards away, 'pass that mallet to the Inspector.'

I must have recycled my bundle of rods three times and still no result. There was just a hint of impatience in his lordship. I could tell he was thinking JCB. Maybe he had suddenly realised who I was, and that his hopes of a happy Christmas were resting on the flea-ridden idiot who had rammed his Roller.

I was thinking that perhaps the terrier had had a fight and lost. For the umpteenth time I rodded and stethoscoped. Despondent, I straightened up, just in time to see a small, dirty, wet, bedraggled, frightened bundle of hair on legs rocket out of a hole, right at the feet of his lordship and straight into his arms.

If the estate workers had been a football team, they had scored in the final minute. Joy was unconfined. Presumably, a lordship under a cloud with her ladyship meant an equal or even greater lack of sunshine for everybody else on the estate, but never mind. The clouds were gone, replaced by glorious rainbows.

Something had trapped the terrier and, somehow, all my mallet banging and rod wiggling had revealed light at the end of the tunnel. A fortunate accident it may have been but, as far as my client was concerned, I was Good King Wenceslas with knobs on. I had never been hugged by a peer of the realm before, and a moment later when her ladyship arrived I was given innumerable noble kisses too.

A happy band trouped back to the big house, the butler was instructed to bring champagne and I was told to name my heart's desire. I thought of asking if the chauffeur could take me in the Roller to the party in York, and wait while I sank a few jars, but I just did my usual 'oh, all in a day's work, don't you know' routine.

A few days later, an enormous hamper full of Harrods goodies arrived at our door, and I had a message from York about an anonymous donation, the biggest single donation they'd seen in years. Thank you, my lord.

7

PERCY THE ELUSIVE PORPOISE

I took a call on Radio Langdale. Carol had had two messages about a dolphin in the river. I thought it was a hoax at first, or a well meaning but short-sighted animal lover who didn't know a dolphin from a salmon. We had some quite big salmon swimming up our river, but they had a purpose and it was the time of year, while it was a hell of a long way upstream for a dolphin to go by accident. But no. These two calls were quite definite. It was a dolphin.

Anything to do with wild animals was always liable to push up through my list of priorities and, just at that moment, there wasn't much else going on so I'd go and have a look at this dolphin. We are in the olden days, remember, without GPS and Google Maps, so I only had a second-hand description of a stretch of the river that was quite out of the way, not really near anywhere populated. This could prove fortunate, if it was a dolphin, because there wouldn't be crowds of people getting easy access to rubberneck and upset it.

I walked up and down the bank for an hour and a half before I saw it, and what a thrill that was. No, it wasn't a dolphin but a very similar, rather smaller animal, a porpoise, a young harbour porpoise in fact, and it was the first time I'd seen one.

Its behaviour didn't seem quite normal, from what I knew. The action of coming out of the water and diving back in is called porpoising, so of course that's what it would do, but not so often, I thought. I watched it for an hour, entranced and undisturbed, knowing that it was in the wrong place and that its future there could only be short term. All kinds of dramatic porpoise rescue scenarios ran through my mind, but I decided that the best thing for the moment would be to leave matters as they were, monitor the situation, and hope that the animal would sort itself out, turn itself round, swim back down the river where it would join the tidal Ouse and thence into the Humber estuary where all Yorkshire rivers end up (except the Tees which, admittedly, is only half Yorkshire – Ed.), and out to the North Sea where it belonged.

At home, I got my animal books out and looked up the porpoise. I knew it was a cetacean, that is, a type of whale, and a toothed one (Odontoceti), and that it was a hunter-predator. I knew what it looked like – triangular dorsal fin, dark grey back, white belly – and that a big threat to the species was being caught up in fishing gear. My books told me that it could dive to more than 600 feet but tended to swim nearer the surface, coming up every half-minute or so to breathe, when it made that sneezing noise I'd heard. Well, I thought, my porpoise was coming up more often than that.

The name came from the Latin *porcus piscis*, which translates as pig fish, but we used to call it by the Anglo-Saxon name *mereswine*, or sea pig, all of which I thought was a bit mean.

They use their own form of sonar echolocation by sending out click sounds that they can read as they bounce back, to locate useful quantities of prey fish but also to communicate with other porpoises. They have good eyesight and much better normal hearing than humans; these are factors that were to play a big part in the story, as was their ability to swim very fast indeed and their shy, elusive nature. In fact, because they are so shy and retiring, not much is known about what they do in the wild.

None of this boded well for a thoroughly domesticated RSPCA inspector brought up on dogs and cats and the occasional alligator, but every day for a week I got up early so I could go and see my new object of fascination. It was a wild animal that had been given a name, something I wouldn't normally go along with, but he was now called

Percy, after the local paper ran a piece on it/him, although we didn't know if he was a Percy or a Priscilla.

As that week went by, Percy increased the frequency of his breathing until he was coming up every few seconds, so I contacted a biologist author I knew of, who lived not far away and had written books on dolphins. He was happy to come with me to see Percy.

His first impressions were not good. Percy, the biologist said, was already suffering from the effects of being in fresh water. The skin was going paler and there were a few small sores on the back and on the dorsal fin. Even so, after some discussion, the decision was to leave it a bit longer and hope nature would resolve matters.

Another week went by of early-morning visits, but things only got worse. If we couldn't get Percy back in the sea soon, he was going to become so sick that he would have to be put down.

I called the fire brigade. All the emergency services were ever willing to help the RSPCA, any time of day or night, and vice versa. We made a plan. A special unit of half a dozen firemen, trained in marine rescue, turned up with a sea-going inflatable boat and a net. We strung the net across the river upstream of Percy, intending to drive him into it, and started the boat's two big engines.

Percy's reaction was immediate. For him, the noise must have been utterly deafening. He disappeared and came up again about 200 yards further up, having dived under our net. We dismantled, re-erected and tried again.

Same result. Tried again, and this time Percy went the other route, leaping right over the top of our net and showing us all what fools we were. After three hours of this, the firemen reluctantly pulled their boat out of the water, shook my hand and wished me the best of British.

I spent the next two days calling every expert I could, in zoos, aquariums, universities, hoping somebody would have a bright idea. Meanwhile, there were numerous voices saying I should do the decent thing and have Percy humanely killed. I knew it might come to that, but not yet.

I rang Geoff, one of my management hierarchy, a senior man based in Sheffield, because I knew he had just acquired a new rescue boat and was the regional leader on such matters. He was delighted at the idea of trying out his new kit and proving it in action and so we, with my old mucker Dan, set about mounting our own rescue.

Plan B was to catch Percy in a much bigger net that we'd had urgently put together from several smaller ones, and pull him into the boat. This boat was not as big as the fire brigade's but the one engine had the same effect, and Percy dashed off, soaring over our trap.

Plan C was to paddle the boat in silence and sneak up on the animal, and that didn't work either. As soon as we got near, off he went, downstream this time, which raised our hopes of chasing him in the right direction, but when we approached again he turned and shot past us upstream.

Up and down the river we went, for miles and hours,

including sliding over a weir, where we almost capsized while Percy proved that he was in his element and we were not. It was exhausting work. He was far too clever for us, and could dive below us out of our sight and stay down for ages. The whole business began to look impossible. I remembered what it said in the books. Shy and retiring nature. Swims very fast. We withdrew to ponder Plan D.

Updates were now appearing every day in the local press, which brought the public to see Percy and helped create a wave of positive interest. Unfortunately, all the informed opinion was against us. Vets, cetacean experts and so on were saying I should call in a marksman and put Percy out of his misery.

Some other marksmen too increased the pressure. I can only assume it was stupid boys, but we saw two small holes in Percy's dorsal fin and what looked like small wounds on his body, doubtless done with an air rifle.

My immediate boss, Fred Sheriff, gave me four more days. If I couldn't effect a rescue, and Percy did not rescue himself, I had to follow the experts and have him destroyed. I knew a man who could do the job, a deer-stalker who was a crack shot and had the right weapon. I was confident that he could deliver the humane bullet, but not if I could help it.

The telly was involved by this stage, with Yorkshire TV's evening news programme, *Calendar*, also running a daily update and speculating on Percy's probable doom. It was turning into a big story and it looked more and more as if it was going to end badly – very badly indeed for Percy, and not so hot for the RSPCA.

At last I had an offer of practical help from the great world of experts, admittedly with a bit of a commercial angle to it but enormously welcome anyway. Flamingo Land zoo was big on dolphin displays, not all that many miles away, near Malton, and a much smaller operation then than it is now. The main dolphin man rang and said he and his team would like to have a go. I explained all that we'd done before and while no new ideas came forth, we agreed we'd have a try anyway.

Dan and Geoff were re-enlisted, and we met up on the river bank at sunrise with two days left of our deadline. The Flamingo Land contingent was something of a surprise, being the general manager, the senior dolphin keeper and the young woman who ran the parrot show, with a small inflatable boat and a pair of oars.

We all looked at Percy and he was in a bad way. His sores were much worse, his skin had a very unhealthy looking pallor, and he was coming up for air more frequently than ever. The dolphin keeper had a grim expression. He'd never seen anything like it. Of course, his dolphins at the zoo were in tip-top condition; the contrast with poor Percy obviously hit home.

We knew that rowing wouldn't work. We'd never got within a hundred yards of the animal before he heard us and dived, so we hatched yet another plan. We used the old narrowboat method of a tow rope, and instead of a horse we had my two RSPCA pals, one on each side of the river, dragging the boat quietly along. More hours went by, and more miles, back and forth as Percy eluded us at will. There was quite a crowd by now, including the telly crew, and we even had some rope-tugging volunteers, but Percy got the better of us as always.

We really were at the point of throwing in the towel, tired, frustrated, defeated, miserable, fed up to the teeth, when we had one last go. Whether Percy was also feeling tired, miserable and fed up we'll never know. Maybe he was disoriented by the noise of the crowd coming from all sides. Whatever the reason, he allowed us – at that moment I was in the boat with the Flamingo Land dolphin man – to creep up on him. I was behind, the dolphin trainer was in the bow, and he leant over and grabbed Percy by the tail.

Percy didn't like it, and in my rush to help I nearly had us all in the water, but I got hold of some bit or other and we pulled him aboard. A smallish one like him should have weighed maybe 45 kilos, or less as he hadn't eaten for a fortnight, but those kilos were all muscle. If you put it in fisherman's terms, we were struggling to get a hold on a 100-pound salmon.

To loud cheers and acclaim, we had him in the boat at last. It was a great moment, and I cannot describe quite how I felt. I'd won the cup, Wimbledon, the Olympics, everything. Then I looked at the dolphin man and he looked at me. We were both thinking the same thing. This much reduced creature we'd caught was too far gone. Percy wasn't going to make it after all.

As well as arranging the sharpshooter, I'd lined up facilities for the best-case scenario, which was a police escort to the nearest seaside town, where two fishing boats and crews were waiting to take Percy out to sea. That was forty miles by road, in my van, out of the water. No chance.

The young woman who ran the Flamingo Land parrot show suddenly turned up with the emergency supplies they'd brought – a tub of lanolin and a pile of blankets. We smeared lanolin all over Percy in an attempt to keep his skin in some sort of condition and to stop him over-heating. The blankets we soaked in the river and covered him with as well as we could, apart from two that we knotted and made into a sling.

By the time we got him to the road and my van, the police were there. We had flashing blue lights in front and behind, and behind that came Flamingo Land, Yorkshire TV, the press and Uncle Tom Cobleigh. We were at the harbour in the shortest possible time, and now our fears started piling up. After days and weeks of fruitless efforts and frustration, everything had gone with mechanical smoothness since the moment we actually caught Percy. It was all too pat. He was breathing fairly well, but he was in such shabby condition that we had horrible thoughts of him slipping into the sea and turning belly up.

Our fishermen friends were keen to help, despite

porpoises not being their natural allies except in the sense that they both like mackerel. One fishing boat was to take the TV crew. The other was to take the RSPCA, Flamingo Land, and Percy.

The first major incident was a fisherman dropping his outboard motor on the foot of the TV presenter, who pressed on regardless of the pain and, we later found out, several broken foot bones.

We were to go about a mile out to sea, which we hoped would be far enough to stop Percy from being really bloody-minded and turning back for the shore. At one point on our way, we hit a couple of breakers and shipped quite a big splash. The sea water seemed to wake Percy up and he began flapping about. Big smiles all round. Everything was going to be all right, wasn't it?

We lowered him over the side in our blanket sling, thinking he might not be strong enough to swim away, or might need a few minutes to acclimatise. Not likely. He thrashed with his tail, ripped the sling from our hands, and disappeared. Twice he surfaced and leapt as he headed for home, and that was the last we saw of him.

8

THE SECRET LIFE OF SERGEANT WAINWRIGHT

We could always expect maximum cooperation from the police, whenever and wherever, but standing out as a six-foot-two, seventeen-stone first among equals was Doug Wainwright. He was almost as animal mad as me, and that surely is saying something. Here's an example.

I had a call from Carol on Radio Langdale that sent me on a scorching August day to a popular beauty spot, a clearing at the edge of some woods near one of our more picturesque villages. There was a river with a small waterfall, a car park and picnic tables. A woman from the village, who had been out walking her dog, had rung in to say that some thoughtless halfwit had left three miniature poodles in a car with no windows open. The windows were steamed up and the dogs seemed in a bad way, and she was specific about the car, a Jaguar saloon in British racing green.

Dogs being left in unventilated cars was a regular occurrence, despite my putting posters up at every tourist car park in the area. Usually, the call from the member of the public was timely enough to save the dog's life, although not to save it from a long period of distress.

It was one of the hottest days of the year. In such weather, inside a car with the windows shut, the temperature rises quickly to an unbearable level. Everybody knows this. Everybody has left a car in sunlight and found it like an oven when they next opened the doors, so why do they leave dogs inside?

When I got there, from what I could see through the condensation on the inside of the windows, one little dog had already collapsed and the other two were nearly gone after their frantic efforts to scratch their way out. No sooner had I taken stock than I was surrounded by picnickers, all seeing what I could see and all telling me I had to do something. I knew Carol had phoned the police but this was an urgent situation, life or death by the look of it, and I didn't think I could afford the time to wait for the law to arrive.

I had no powers to break into a car but I was working out how I might do it when good old Sergeant Wainwright turned up, only minutes after me, siren going and blue light flashing.

'Can you get to the door handle through the quarter-light?' I suggested.

'Bollocks to that,' said Doug. 'Let the ignorant ****house pay for a back window.'

So he took out his truncheon and with one blow smashed the back window into tiny pieces – no alarms on cars in those days. One dog was laid out on the shelf above the back seat, and it was dead, well beyond help. Another was collapsed on the seat, and the third was half sitting, supported by the car door. We grabbed the two living dogs and ran to the waterfall with them.

We gave them a good ducking in the cold water, which might have been too much of a shock but that was a risk we had to take. One came round in a minute or two as if from a trance, with its eyes glazed over as it staggered around in the shallow pool. The other took a bit longer to come back from the dead; neither of them could walk properly. I opened up my van and laid them in the back under a wet blanket.

Quite soon after, the owners arrived. We knew it was them because the man, seeing the state of his car from fifty yards away, started shouting abuse. He was a coarse, very fat, red-faced oaf from – well, let's just say the West Riding conurbation, accompanied by a peroxide-blonde lady, his wife going by the size and number of rings on her left hand, well bejewelled elsewhere, tight-sweatered, leopard-skin trousered and stiletto-heeled, something like Marina off *Last of the Summer Wine* only nowhere near as charming. Goodness knows where they'd been. They didn't look like birdwatchers.

The man seemed used to everyone jumping when he spoke, but he hadn't met Sergeant Wainwright before, who got his retaliation in first. Anyone stopped by the police in the olden days will know that the first thing they said was 'Is this your car, sir?'; now of course they say, 'Is this your car, mate?' Doug Wainwright said, 'Is this your car, you fat bastard?'

The oaf began blustering about how he couldn't be talked to like that, and Sergeant Wainwright let him run on for a bit, then told him he was under arrest for animal cruelty and got the handcuffs out and pushed his arm up his back. I tried to calm things down but Doug told me to belt up, cautioned the man and offered several charges including killing one of his dogs.

The woman burst into tears and was still sobbing, in between calling her husband various names, as Doug put them in the police car and drove off. I did the same, heading for the vet's, where one dog was dehydrated enough to be put on a saline drip. Once I knew that the two animals were in a stable condition, I set off for the cop shop where I found Doug having a cup of tea. He was in no rush to interview the errant couple but eventually we did that together, when it turned out that madam was a real poodle enthusiast, used to be a breeder, now just went around the shows including Cruft's. She was distraught, while he was still in a fury about his car, wrecked by this monster who called himself a policeman.

At that remark, if Doug had socked him one I shouldn't have been surprised, but I think he was now feeling sorry for the woman, clearly desolated by what had happened and, for her sins, married to this crass cretin.

They pleaded guilty at the magistrates' court to three charges of animal cruelty under the 1911 Act and were fined £200 on each count, which was a considerable sum then, maybe equivalent to a total of £3,000 today.

Doug Wainwright was a legend, a fearless copper of the old school whose breed has disappeared from British policing under the weight of modernisation. I'd heard a couple of stories about him from way back, when he was a PC in a certain Yorkshire seaside town.

One day, he bid good morning to a man who was well known to the police but who wasn't engaged in criminal activity at that moment and so, in Doug's view, was entitled to civility. As Doug walked on, he heard the man say something extremely derogatory to his girlfriend, about the local constabulary as currently represented, so he strolled back to the man, who was sitting on the harbour wall. Checking that the tide was out, Doug gave the man a mighty push that sent him backwards into the mud below.

Complaints from a known villain would never get anywhere with the station inspector then, and the same applied in the tale of the electric colander. Another well-known felon, a burglar by trade, had been arrested for being drunk and disorderly. There were several burglaries on the books that the police knew this man had done but they couldn't prove it, so Doug said he would get a confession.

This burglar was a little ferret of a chap, thoroughly disreputable, and still fairly drunk, so he didn't question anything when Doug and a colleague took him to the interview room, put a colander from the station kitchen on his head, and connected it to a radiator with a set of jump leads. Doug took out a walkie-talkie radio and told the deeply confused suspect that here they had the very latest in lie detectors. He would turn the device on with his radio, and ask some specific questions about a recent series of burglaries. If the man told a lie, the detector would give him a painful electric shock.

All the cases were cleared up without recourse to electricity.

In one way, Doug Wainwright was an orthodox animal nut, very knowledgeable, interested in everything, but in another he was somewhat eccentric. His speciality was reptiles, but he would have mini-crazes on particular species and he would have to have the experience of keeping them. Here was a man who could name every kind of snake in the Latin, but who also got excited about trying to tame a weasel. There was even a story from his earlier times by the seaside that he'd tried to tame a seal into going swimming with him.

Over the years, he actually became something of a national expert on reptiles although he had no academic background. Just his enthusiasm that took him into every corner and every source of information.

He rang me one day with that familiar tone in his voice that always made me think, Now what's he done? He had acquired a boa constrictor, about ten feet long, as thick as your leg, and I had to go round to see it. I could tell it was too late for a lecture on the dangers of keeping large constrictors and, anyway, I thought, Doug knew what he was doing.

He had it in a massive vivarium and, I have to say, it was a most impressive creature, but over the next few weeks Doug became increasingly concerned. I didn't know where he'd got the snake from and I didn't ask, and he didn't seem to know when it had last fed, and it was not at all interested in the dead rats Doug was offering. Constrictors don't need to eat very often, but after three months Doug decided he had to do more to tempt it. He took it out of the vivarium, thinking perhaps that if he could get a rat in its mouth it would swallow it.

We think of these giants being able to dislocate their jaws so they can swallow prey animals bigger than themselves that they've just crushed to death. We've seen pictures of a snake with a large bulge where the last meal is being digested. All true, but what perhaps we don't realise is that a big constrictor has a big mouth anyway, maybe fifteen inches across and, although it doesn't live by striking with a venomous bite, it can do that without the venom.

This constrictor clearly didn't like being handled by Doug, and it struck at him. It bit him on the face, and he had tooth marks in a circle, across his forehead, down his cheeks, and under his nose. How it missed his eyes we shall never know. Face covered in blood, he pushed his pet snake back into its vivarium and went to A & E at the nearest hospital.

He was well known in there. He often ended up bringing drunks in who had glassed each other or some such, but he was not in uniform this time and he looked like he'd been glassed himself. The nurses didn't recognise him.

They listened to his story, but didn't entirely believe it. I got a rather weird call from the hospital, saying that there was a very dodgy character who had been mistreating snakes and could I call by. Which I did, and the staff nurse repeated her suspicions, that this man might be a snake dealer, perhaps selling them for meat, or importing them illegally, and he'd obviously been doing something bad for the snake to bite him like that.

I said I'd stroll by the cubicle and see what I could see, and I had some difficulty not bursting out laughing when I saw a disconsolate Doug sitting there, looking like an extra from *The Curse of the Mummy's Tomb*, blood seeping through the bandages that swathed his head.

I told the nurse that she had been quite right to call me, and I needed to interview this suspect snake-charmer at the police station to get to the bottom of it. I then popped in to see Doug, almost choked trying not to laugh, while he asked me for a lift home as he'd walked there. I escorted him from the premises, tipping a wink to the staff nurse, and that was that, except it wasn't.

A few weeks later, Doug happened to mention going into Casualty with his injured drunks to be stitched up, and how friendly the nurses had always been, cracking jokes and generally trying to make the night shift go with a swing. 'That was until recently,' he said. 'I don't know what I've done but they won't talk to me now.'

9

THE WAR NOBODY WINS

When an inspector took over a new territory, the first thing to do was study a very variable document called Branch Hints. If the previous incumbent had been diligent and efficient, the Hints could be comprehensive with loads of helpful stuff – maps, lists of contacts in the police and fire brigade, recommended vets, not so recommended vets, RSPCA supporters, committee members, market days, good pubs, everything that might be useful – plus the baddies. These were known offenders and reoffenders, who you would find yourself going back to again and again, to check on their animals.

Contained in my Branch Hints, when I first moved to Scorswick, were a couple of paragraphs about a gypsy family. These were not the type of traveller you see nowadays at Appleby New Fair, with their massive, flash, chromium-plated caravans complete with family silver and satellite dish, pulled by the biggest, ugliest four-wheel drives. No, these were the traditional sort, living in horse-drawn, bowtop wagons and not, seemingly, having any particular occupation nor ready source of income.

My father would have called them didicois, the rough-and-ready gypsy lower classes (Romany word *dikakai* – 'look here, man', what you see is what you get), who followed the travelling ways. Such a lifestyle was feasible in the latter half of the nineteenth and first half of the twentieth centuries. Families could follow a circuit, stopping here and there, same places at the same time every year, to do occasional farm work, buy, sell and train horses, do whatever odd jobs there were, mend things, tell fortunes, sell cheap herbal remedies to people who couldn't afford a doctor, pick up scrap metal, and move on.

There was trouble sometimes, but generally it was live and let live. Country folk in those days would not dial 999 to complain about a gypsy woman drying her washing on the hedge.

Now there is no market for the travellers' crafts and services. There is no potato picking, we don't mend pans any more, we don't believe in the powers of lucky white heather, and the few people who keep horses prefer the vet's antibiotics to the gypsies' magic medicine. A lot of the old gypsy families have moved on to new trades – loft insulation, driveway asphalting, landscape gardening, second-hand cars – but these gypsies of mine had not done that. They had kept to the old ways, without the old ways of making it work.

They never went anywhere. They might move to the other end of the lane where there was some grass for their horses, and back again later, but that was it. They were non-travelling travellers, and the reason for it I guessed was the old man, the patriarch, Tom he was called, who seemed to spend his entire existence sitting outside on a log, beside the fire that was always burning, looking into the embers.

Reading what was in the Hints, and noting the number of complaints my predecessor had taken, accusing them of poor treatment of horses and dogs, I decided to take the friendly approach and get to know these people. There were eight of them. The seniors were Old Tom – although how old I could never tell, maybe sixty, maybe ninety – and a very jolly, well-rounded lady called Meg who might have been his wife but could have been his daughter or younger sister. In any case, she was always telling him to do something or other, which he never did.

There were three more women, one about seventeen, one about thirty, and one in between who had the looks to be a film star: underneath the grime, the tangled hair, the dirty rags of clothes, there was a dark-eyed Hollywood beauty.

There were two men, who would have been the bread-winners had any bread been won, and little Joe, seven years old. Joe was the pride and joy of the family. Every week day in term time, somebody from social services picked him up, took him somewhere, stripped him, showered him, put him in primary school uniform, and dropped him off at school. At the end of the day, the procedure was reversed, without the shower.

Little Joe was the first member of the clan to receive a normal education and so would be the first to be able to write. Gypsies often claim to be unable to read, although I've never seen one having any difficulty with the racing pages, and their mental arithmetic when working out a deal would leave me standing, but little Joe would still be unique in that he would be a master of all three of the Rs.

Because their camp was only a short detour from my usual route into the office, I became a regular visitor. I can't say I was ever totally accepted, but certainly the family, and patriarch Tom especially, went from fairly sullen mistrust to friendly tolerance, apart maybe from one of the men, and when I gave Tom my old uniform tunic he was genuinely delighted and never took it off. I kept a close eye on their horses and their lurcher dogs, and all was well.

I used my veterinary contacts to get a free supply of medicines so I could inject any new dogs against distemper, and got treatments for the horses too. And, because our own son Carter junior was just a bit older than little Joe, there were clothes cast-offs. If my small rescue shelter in the potting shed was low on canine customers, there would be excess dog food I could pass on, and so we went over two years and more.

My visits gradually became less frequent as I believed the need grew less, and I had plenty of other business to attend to. One very cold winter's day, I decided to look in. I pulled up to have a chat with the van window down, when I saw something that immediately overcame my reluctance to get out in the freezing air. It looked like a dead dog, attached by baler twine to a wooden peg but hidden under one of the wagons. I could only just see it and, clearly, I was not supposed to. The gypsies saw that I'd seen and went into a guilty panic.

'Don't you look at that, sir, it's nothing. Nothing at all to worry about. Don't you go troubling about that, boss,' and so on. Of course I did have to go troubling, and what I found shocked me greatly. I had believed these people were doing right by their animals, and that our friendship and mutual trust had put another layer of good will on top of that.

I pulled on the string and looked down on a scene of horror. It had been a lurcher, and it was the most emaciated creature I had ever come across. There was no flesh on its bones at all. It had been suffering horribly from demodectic mange, it was covered in sores, and I couldn't tell how long it had been dead.

I blew my top at them. How could they do this? What could possess them to be so cruel to a dog that had been bred to serve them? Maybe it was one I'd injected, I didn't know. Well, there wouldn't be any more injections because there wouldn't be any more dogs. I'd get them into court and they'd be banned from keeping dogs.

They just stood there, not saying anything, not offering any kind of explanation. I looked hard at the one family member who had never lost his mistrust of me, a man of about forty known as Young Tom, presumably son of, and he wouldn't meet my eye.

'It's yours, isn't it, Tom?' I said. I could see the women were furious with him and, under such pressure, he nodded, and then they turned on me, pleading with me to let it go. They would bury the dog and nobody need know any more about it.

This I could not do. Not only was it my job; it was the worst case of animal abuse I had seen. I asked Young Tom to get into my van.

The procedure for an interview in those days followed Judges' Rules. You issued a caution, same as the police, you do not have to say anything but anything you do say, and so on, and then asked your questions. You wrote down both question and answer in your notebook, and that was that. Young Tom did not have to sign, not that he would have done anyway, and not that it mattered because he took quite literally the bit about not having to say anything.

He would not tell me how long he'd had the dog, what he did with it, why it was in such a terrible state, nothing. I had a list of questions in my book with no answers, except he did admit it was his dog and he had never taken it to a vet.

Well, that was the first thing I did, and my vet friend, the one who gave me the free vaccines, could hardly believe his eyes either. His post-mortem found no subcutaneous fat so the conclusion was that the animal had died of starvation, a verdict made even more painful by the discovery of bits of chewed up plastic. The poor thing had eaten its food bowl.

I went back and told Young Tom that I was going to report him. The case, I thought, was open and shut. We had my notebook, a set of photographs, the vet's statement as expert witness, and the accused's admission of ownership. The photographs had been taken by a police scenes-of-crime officer, when I took the body to the police station, and they were highly professional.

RSPCA headquarters agreed to a prosecution and I had to serve the summons. Needless to say, the family's attitude to me had changed somewhat. They were united around Young Tom and I was the devil incarnate, to be abused, spat at, and cursed to the ends of the earth. The summons was torn up, rolled into a ball and thrown on the fire. I told them the time and date of the hearing, and the likely consequences of non-appearance thereat, and left, not believing for a moment that Young Tom would turn up unassisted.

I went and got him myself. Goodness me, he was a scruffy sod. The smell was awful, and I guessed (correctly)

I should need the Nuvan Top again. He pleaded guilty, the magistrates studied the evidence, and I shan't forget the looks of revulsion on their faces when they saw the photographs. They retired to discuss sentencing. When they returned the chairman of the bench – not, on this occasion, my favourite viscount – had thought carefully about what to say.

'It is in my power to send you to prison,' he said, 'where prisoners and warders alike will find out what you've done and make your life hell. The preferred course of action is to have you taken to the market place and flogged, but unfortunately that is not an option. After due consideration, we have decided to ban you for life from keeping dogs, and to fine you £300.'

In those days £300 was a lot of money, and an astronomical sum for somebody like Young Tom. I doubt if the magistrates believed there was anything in gypsy curses because otherwise, after a short speech from Tom, they could not have expected to see the next morning.

None of the family ever spoke to me again except to curse and swear and threaten to get me a season ticket to A & E. I kept my visits to the camp to a necessary minimum, avoiding aggro by checking first to make sure the family was out, but I couldn't avoid contact entirely. One day I was at my dog shelter, with Carol and the children, when the whole lot of them turned up. The abuse was pretty vile and Carol bundled the kids into my van and got in herself.

I stood there and took it, knowing that the knives

wouldn't really come out, when a cop car arrived, blue light flashing, and my friend Sergeant Wainwright and an equally bulky PC sent the gypsies on their way. I asked the sarge how he happened to be passing, and he said not at all, they'd had a call from a member of the public.

Carol had a slightly embarrassed look on her face.

'Yes, well,' she said, 'you've just had this new radio fitted, so I thought I'd better learn how to work it.'

10

HOW TO MAKE A FIREMAN LAUGH

If you took the charitable view on the way some travellers treat their horses, you might use the word 'carelessly'. I know many RSPCA inspectors who would use stronger language than that, including me, but careless happens to suit this particular story.

The type of horse much favoured by the traveller community is the fell pony, often brown and white, with a big creamy mane and big feet, which they call a coloured horse and which, in the old days, was considered the ideal motive power for a living wagon, a caravan, which would generally weigh around a ton. For one horse to pull a ton for hours at a time, it needed to be built for work, and that's what these fell ponies are, strong, powerful, of a quiet but determined nature.

Some travellers had stopped on the roadside, quite a way out of Scorswick. They had coloured horses but not to pull their caravans, which were of the flash, chromium-plated variety. They had vehicles to do that, and to carry the horses, and the animals were obviously glad to have a bit of grazing even if it was beside a busy road.

Whenever anything like this happened, my phone would start ringing, often from well-meaning but inexpert people who assumed that the horses were being poorly looked after. Sometimes, maybe often, that was the case, but not this time. I went to have a look at the half-dozen or so ponies they had and all looked fit and well.

Still the phone kept ringing, and one call had me jumping in my van right away. 'A little brown and white horse' had been seen by such-and-such a wood, apparently entangled in something and in trouble. The place was several miles from the travellers' camp, but I had no doubt about what the animal was and whence it came, and certainly the word 'careless' was one of several that occurred to me as I drove there.

It took me a while to find the pony because by this time, exhausted by its struggles, it had lain down in the long grass on the edge of the wood, at the top of a steep slope. Goodness knows how it had got itself into such a mess, but it was tangled in wire – not barbed wire, but single-strand fencing wire that had been in a tight coil and so, when released, had sprung into curls and hoops that had wrapped around the body and one of the back legs of this horse. The animal was also still attached to the source of its distress, with wire heading off into the woods and out of sight.

I thought I had the complete tool kit for every rescue eventuality – all kinds of nets, graspers, poles, things for keeping animals at a distance, things for bringing them closer, but the one thing I didn't have was any kind of cutter mighty enough to deal with this wire. If I couldn't cut it, I would have to untie it.

It was a winter's day, cold and gloomy, and my hands were soon blue. I couldn't wear gloves and manipulate the wire but, after a good hour and more had passed, I felt I had made some progress. Covered in mud and freezing I may have been, but I had managed to uncoil some of the wire from the back leg and the body.

The pony thought I had done even better than that, because it got up and dashed for freedom. It didn't get far before it was brought to ground again and, frustrated, it began to twist and turn about. In my attempts to help, in among thrashing hooves and springing wire that did everything I didn't want it to do, I was soon enmeshed. The pony and I were trapped together in a metal spider's web that had a tortuous will of its own.

The more the pony struggled, the tighter gripped the coils of wire around me. I had one arm free, but that was no use. In such situations, a resigned attempt at a smile might turn into hysterical laughter or, in my case, a wild imagining of what would happen to me if the pony managed to get up and charge for the woods, dragging me behind it like something out of a cowboy film.

It was more than brawny enough to do that. Man might have dominion over the beasts of the field, but strength-wise it's no contest. I remembered watching a farrier shoeing one of these particular beasts in a farmyard. He'd hitched it to a full-size metal farm gate. While he went into the barn to find something, the horse lifted the gate off its hinges and, panicking, whirled around with the gate like a hammer-thrower in the Olympics, and whacked the farrier's van with it.

Every attempt to loosen and undo the wire was met by more horse movement and I was getting nowhere. Daylight was disappearing and the temperature was dropping even further. I could see the headlines: 'Man and Horse Found Frozen to Each Other'.

For want of a simple pair of bolt cutters, my glittering career was over. Well, they say that going slowly unconscious with hypothermia is not a painful way to pass beyond, to that great animal sanctuary in the sky.

And then the miracle happened. The fire brigade arrived. The first man on the scene was a lad I knew well, and he just stood there, laughing and laughing. The rest of the crew joined in. The woods and fields rang with jolly firemen's guffaws.

'Two animals to rescue at once,' said one, and that set them off again. 'The woman on the phone, she just said horse. Never mentioned RSPCA man.' More hilarity.

At last their kindly natures took over. They fetched their bolt cutters and set us both free. This story, I thought, will run and run, and so it did. Every time I called the brigade out to help me rescue an animal, I was asked how many animals were involved, and if that number included me.

The firemen collected up all the wire and took it away. I checked the pony and, apart from a few sore places on its legs, it was fine once it had had a good drink. I knew there was no point in trying to find out exactly who had been careless enough to let this horse wander and get into bother. Its owner, or owners, would deny any knowledge. Not my horse, boss. No idea. Never seen it before.

All I could do was tether it in a safe place where there was grazing. I would pop by to keep tabs and top up its water, and one day very soon it would disappear as if by magic, and reappear in the travellers' company. There was no risk in this strategy. Good heavens, I was an experienced inspector; I knew better than to get tangled in an argument about gypsy horses. I knew exactly what would happen, and it did. I went to the ironmonger's and bought a good pair of bolt cutters.

11

MY LIFE WITH BADGERS

It had been a fairly quiet week with nothing out of the ordinary at all, then the Highways Department rang to tell me that a busy main road was about to collapse and would I kindly do something about it, and quick. Badgers had made a sett in the road embankment and, keen to explore territory on the other side, had dug tunnels or bedrooms or something and seriously undermined the road, just at the point where it took a sharpish bend, to the stage where the county surveyor had declared it unsafe and set up a diversion. This diversion was greatly inconvenient and unsuitable for the large amount of traffic so, as already stated, would I sort the matter out?

Somebody in the highways office must have known that RSPCA inspectors had a general licence to disturb badger setts and take away matter therefrom, which of course was (and is) illegal otherwise, apart from an exception at that time that allowed fox hunters to stop up setts temporarily to prevent foxes escaping into them. We had this licence so we could gather evidence in court cases. It did not give us a free hand to stop badgers digging under main roads but that's what the highways people wanted me to do.

I didn't know this particular sett but we were in February, the middle of the badger breeding season, so I thought I'd better take a badger expert with me for a second opinion on whatever we might find.

It was not a big sett, quite small in fact, but that in itself is no sure guide. My badger-expert friend and I had both seen huge setts with only two or three mature animals at home, and small ones with eight or nine, but this we thought looked like a fairly minor installation although very active. There were three or four holes and plenty of spoil heaps, well-worn paths to and from, but no signs of breeding such as extra bedding being brought in.

The highways people suggested blocking the badgers in, and/or gassing them. I told them they couldn't do that. In which case, they said, I had better dig them out, perhaps by tomorrow.

One of the main reasons for the badger laws is to make digging them up illegal. As far as I knew, nobody had ever been given a permit to get around this law, and when I contacted the Ministry of Agriculture, I could tell I was giving them a new puzzle to solve. The response was that, since I already had the general licence to disturb and take away, I might be given a further, special licence, but they would need to consider the case and put forward a recommendation to the government minister responsible.

The highways officials couldn't see (a) why a few hairy animals could cause such disruption, (b) why the Min of Ag as a government department couldn't understand the urgency of the matter, and (c) why they in the county highways office should have to take a continuous stream of complaints from people living in villages, hitherto peaceful, now suffering the mighty roar of main-road traffic on diversion.

Meanwhile, I had to make plans on the assumption that I would, or would not, get my special licence. My first idea was to cross to the dark side to consult another kind of expert, not actually a badger digger but a well-known local poacher. He suggested making purse nets, bigger versions of the ones he used for rabbiting. The badgers would bolt from the sett via their usual tunnels, and bingo.

The problem with this idea was how to make them bolt. Digging alone wouldn't work, which we couldn't do anyway, because the badgers would almost certainly respond by digging themselves further in. The only way would be to put a dog into the sett, which might work if the badger had never experienced it before, but if it had, it wouldn't flee. It would face the foe and there would be a fight.

So, that was a non-starter. We needed more information on our sett and so mounted an all-night vigil, taking turns with some local badger enthusiasts, one of whom, called Jennie, rather stood out from the usual run of wildlifers as, to my mind, someone who had perhaps starred as a Bond girl. We did this for three nights and never saw a badger, while during the days I had the highways getting more and more aggravated, demanding action, and the ministry telling me that no decision had been made yet.

What to do with the badgers, should we ever get hold of them, was also a pressing matter, and our solution was to build an artificial sett. The technology of such a thing is well understood now, but then there was no information available so we had to make up our own technology. The modern way is to build an underground cavern with breeze blocks, with several entrances and a surrounding fence. What we did was persuade a farmer to dig a great hole a couple of fields away and bury a metal water tank in it, in which we'd cut a couple of openings. This we managed in just one day, so that was something that went well.

Next up was a self-proclaimed animal rights activist from town, who said he knew a lot more about badgers than we did and who objected, very noisily and regularly, to anything and everything that we attempted or thought of attempting. I did know him slightly, as I'd heard stories about his failed efforts to rear fox cubs and rehabilitate them. Not that he had a reasonable answer to our current problem. For him, the right of the badgers to dig wherever they wanted was paramount, and let the main road collapse if that happened to be the consequence. He was a nuisance, and was portrayed as such in the press who were now well onto the case. Jennie told him to something off out of it, with no result as he was impervious even to that.

At last, after five days and nights, I got my licence to dig from the ministry. We met at dawn – me, five volunteers including Bond girl Jennie, the highways people, the police, and a JCB with driver. Also there was our animal rights man, who lay down across the entrance to the sett prepared, as he loudly proclaimed, to die rather than have the badgers dug out.

Sergeant Wainwright, always on hand when it was something to do with animals, arrested the fellow for causing a breach of the peace and had him removed from the scene, and the digging began. Our driver was a top man at the job, and he started removing the soil from the embankment as carefully as an archaeologist with a spoon. We took it in turns to kneel beside the digger bucket, watching for any sign of a badger.

We'd kept the nets over the exit holes, hoping that the animals would flee when the JCB got going, but that didn't happen and the digger man carried on all day. We found plenty of badger evidence – bracken bedding, their internal latrine they used in bad weather – and we had to conclude that, rather than run for it, they had decided to dig for it, in which case there had to come a point when they, superior high-speed diggers though they were, would be outdug by our man with JCB.

Dusk was gathering about us. The JCB had its lights on. On and on we went until, at last, Jennie on kneeler duty spotted a piece of badger. The soil was cleared around it – it wasn't going anywhere, having adopted its standard defence position of curling into a ball with its head between its front legs – and I set to with my grasper. A curled-up, motionless and decidedly grumpy badger must be the most difficult animal to grasp and it took me a good half an hour before I managed it.

This was a fine, healthy female that we popped into a cat basket before, in the encircling gloom, we set about finding her mate. That came about quite quickly and the highways department was happy. We of the badger fraternity were happy too but exhausted after our long nights of vigil and so decided to leave the animals in their baskets overnight and release them into the artificial sett in the morning.

Of course, this would be a new experience for us and the badgers, and we made plans based on common sense and standard practice when moving large animals, such as pigs, although the lack of a bucket full of nosh would be a hindrance. We would place the cat basket next to the hole, so that the badger could see a darkness at the end of the tunnel, and we would make that tunnel very short, with sides and roof of hardboard sheets. We chose to do the male first.

Badgers have a better power-to-weight ratio than any rock climber, and I'd only got the cat basket lid half open before he thrust his way through our feeble construction and was off. I have to say that I'd have let him go. Not only was he a very muscular body athlete; he was a highly competent butcher, and one bite from him could quite literally have had your hand off.

Our badger volunteer had no such fears. Jennie proved herself a Bond girl in more ways than one, as she moved like lightning, grabbed Brock around his middle and stuffed him in the hole before you could say bloody Nora. I was speechless; Jennie obviously thought she'd just done what anybody would have done.

The sow badger was treated with more respect, with extra hands holding on to the hardboard, and she went in with no trouble at all. It took three of us to roll the boulder into place to block the entrance, so we felt fairly confident that two badgers couldn't shift it, experienced as they might be at lifting stones out of the way so they can dig up wasp nests.

They would stay there for a week, until the road embankment had been reconstructed, this time with a tunnel through that allowed the badgers to follow their instincts and search for food without crossing the road which, I think, was the first time anybody had done this. Certainly it was the first I'd heard of such a thing.

The old sett had been completely demolished, with no further badgers found. The animal rights chap wrote to the local paper saying we'd left badger cubs to die, but this was drivel, and the paper gave the full and true story plenty of coverage.

The volunteers and I took it in turns over three weeks to monitor the badger traffic and everything seemed to go well. I can also say that, ten years later, our primitive converted water tank had become a thriving badger colony, active and growing, with full use being made of the tunnel, and, as far as I know, it still is.

Badger hunting and baiting – staging fights with terriers – have been popular pursuits for centuries, all over Europe and elsewhere. In Germany, they even produced a specific breed of dog:

the dachshund – 'badger hound' – developed to go into badgers' tunnels to flush them out. Baiting was made illegal in Britain in 1835, not that that made much difference, and badger protection will remain a big part of an RSPCA inspector's workload.

*

Although the RSPCA provided me with a house, there was no extra facility on the premises, purpose made, for an animal hospital and residential care home, which is what RSPCA inspectors tend to end up needing.

So, as well as my potting shed in town, I had refitted our garage, full of all sorts and sizes of cage, basket and box, largely empty in the winter when the wild world tends to stay at home, but thronged in the summer with orphans and injured. We had everything in there, songbirds, oiled seabirds sometimes that I used to clean up in our bath, fox cubs, bats, rabbits, birds of prey . . . but not bears as our neighbour thought when he mis-overheard me talking about an injured hare.

'You can't keep bears in there. This is a residential area,' he said as he stormed off to phone the police.

Occasionally a badger would be brought in – I say occasionally because these are nocturnal animals and their clashes with humankind are usually fatal. When a badger is caught in the headlights, it will tend to adopt one of two responses. It might stand its ground, dazzled, but facing the threat. Or, it will curl into a ball, its tough, rubbery skin being a good defence against most enemies but not much use against a speeding motor car.

On one occasion I had a youngish badger that I guess had curled and only taken a glancing blow, because all it had suffered was a minor fracture to one shoulder. The vet said it would recover fully; I was to keep it comfortable for a few weeks then release it back into the wild.

I could have done just that, but no, I had to use this elusive animal for educational purposes. It was part of our remit, to spread the word and try to prevent cruelty and ill-treatment at source, by going into schools, youth clubs and so on. In rural areas there were always those activities loosely associated with hunting – cubbing, for instance, digging out fox cubs for terriers to kill – and there was always badger digging and baiting – out of sight, known only to the chosen few, but it was there and still is.

Most people never see a badger except as roadkill; children, not generally nocturnal in their habits, will certainly never have been close to one. Maybe I could get the local kids on-side before one of the most unpleasant rural traditions took a hold. Maybe they might have an influence at home.

Our village primary school was like thousands around the country – two point four teachers, thirty- nine pupils, two classes, with a vague threat of closure always hanging over it – but this one was slightly different for me because my two children went to it, and I knew the teachers very well. The head, Miss Keeble, a superb exemplar to her profession, was a bit worried about me bringing a badger into school but I reassured her that there was no possibility of anything untoward happening. In fact, so reassured was she that, thinking a bit of publicity would do the school no harm, she invited the local press to attend the unique wildlife experience that was to be me and my badger.

I had it all planned. I would give a short talk on the wildlife in the area, ask the children a few easy questions, and then bring out my surprise exhibit and let them look at the badger in its cage, which was a large cat basket.

My talk was based around wild animals that had come to me in my work, and that I'd photographed. Most of them had a bit of a story to them, and I could ask the children if they recognised this bird – a buzzard – or that animal – a stoat – and if they knew anything about them.

Of course I was anxious not to let Carter and Kate show their superior knowledge of the subject, which they were bound to have being in my family, but I was equally anxious that they shouldn't show me up, so I had carefully dropped a few subtle hints into the conversation the night before.

'I had a look at that badger earth this morning,' I said to Carol over tea.

'Don't you mean badger sett? It's foxes that live in earths, surely.'

'Sorry, I meant sett.' And so on.

My other tactic was in the classroom, to ignore my own children's upstretched hands as much as possible when I asked each question, until I'd been round everybody and could ignore them no longer.

'What do we call the place where badgers live?'

'Dad, Dad, I know, I know, I know.'

Miss Keeble interrupted here, to tell Carter junior, then aged about seven, that Carter senior was, this afternoon, Inspector, not Dad.

'Sorry, Miss. Inspector, I know.'

'All right then. Where does a badger live?'

'In a hole! It is. They do. Why are you all laughing?'

One lad, a farmer's son, put his hand up and told us.

'It's a sett. A badger sett. You should ask your dad what it's called.'

The embarrassment was not going to end there.

'All right. Where do rabbits live?'

I was surprised that only three or four hands went up. One was the farmer's son's, and one was daughter Kate's, then aged nine.

'Me. Me, I know, I know, Dad.'

'Inspector,' said Miss Keeble.

'Sorry, Miss. Anyway, I know, I know.'

'All right, Kate. Where do rabbits live?'

'In a hutch!'

It took some time for order to be restored. I felt that Miss Keeble could have moved a little more quickly to quell the glee, though I was pleased she asked another pupil rather than that farmer's son again, so she could write 'warren' on the blackboard.

Never mind. I was confident that my badger would retrieve the situation. I told them that I had a special surprise, an animal that I doubted any of them had seen alive before, and I was sure they'd never been close to. I told them it had been knocked over by a car but was on the mend, I was going to release it next week so this was their last and only chance to see one, but also they had to keep quiet. A lot of noise could frighten the animal and that is not what we do.

I went out to my van and came back with the cat basket covered in a black cloth. I was going to do a Tommy Cooper and whisk the cloth away, to reveal my prize exhibit. The audience, all the children in the school around the table, two teachers and the local press photographer, waited in tense anticipation.

I took the cloth off and of course they didn't keep quiet. There were Oohs and Aahs, chatter, excited little voices squeaking, and it was a while before Miss Keeble and I could get them quiet enough to file past the basket in pairs, to peer inside and get a good look at Mr Brock.

When all had stood and stared, it was the kids' turn to ask questions. Can he kill a fox, how many of them live in the hole (very funny, thank you), what does he eat (maybe a hundred worms a night, super-disgust all round), does he bite?

No, he doesn't bite, well, not people anyway. Badgers are shy, retiring animals, wary of humans, and keen to keep out of our way. They will never have a go at you like the Scottie dog bites the postman.

This would not do for the farmer's son. He'd bet that the badger would bite, and he'd bet that it would eat all sorts of things, and he'd bet that it would hunt and bite and bite whatever it could.

'No, no, that's not right,' said I. 'Look at him. He's frightened of you, curled up in a ball. He thinks you might bite him, not the other way around. Look, I'll show you.'

Rushing in where angels would have rapidly backpedalled, I undid the catch on the basket and slowly lifted the lid. Mr Brock didn't even twitch. I waved my hand slowly over him.

I'd been reading *Albert and the Lion* as a bedtime

story the other night. 'Now Albert had heard about lions, how they was ferocious and wild. To see Wallace lying so peaceful, Well, it didn't seem right to the child. So straightway the brave little feller, Not showing a morsel of fear, Took his stick with the 'orse's 'ead 'andle, And pushed it in Wallace's ear.'

Well, my badger lay in a somnolent posture like Wallace the lion, only I wasn't going to push my stick in his ear. I was doing healing gestures. See? I told you he wouldn't bite me.

Badgers have this special ability to uncoil from their ball in an instant and lash out with their fearsome teeth, which they will do when attacked by a terrier to go upwards for its throat. They have a different sort of jaw arrangement to most mammals, which means that once they lock on, they are almost impossible to prise off. They're as fast as a striking snake when they do this, but I saw him coming and, instead of him grabbing my whole hand he only managed to rip a deep furrow across the back of it, leaving me with a scar for life.

I could not have arranged anything more exciting for the children, unless the badger had actually bitten my hand right off. There was blood everywhere, the press photographer's flash gun was going at disco speed, Miss Keeble was running around with a first-aid kit, and the farmer's boy was shouting, 'I told you, I told you' across the rest of the mayhem.

Miss Keeble wanted to take me to hospital but I

couldn't face even more embarrassment. Tell me, Mr Langdale, how did you get this? Really? You put your hand in the cage?

'It's only a scratch,' I said to Miss Keeble, about something that needed stitches, and proceeded to dig myself further into my own sett by pointing out to the children how quick the badger had been, and what a good educational lesson they'd had.

12

HOLIDAYS OF
A LIFETIME

The great downside of being an RSPCA inspector was lack of time with the kids. I know a lot of fathers will say the same, but mine was frequently a seven-days-a-week job, and far more often than not I was up and away in the morning before Carter Junior and Kate were out of bed, and back too late for a bedtime story. Once they got to the sort of age where I could be trusted to look after them, we formed a tradition. I would take the two of them away for a week's holiday, while Carol shut up shop and went off somewhere pleasant for her own rest and recuperation.

Of course, I also wanted to go somewhere pleasant, and my idea of that was camping out in the wild and woolly wilderness – and it was real camping too, bivvy bags beneath the stars, not luxury tents and camp beds. My children tell me now that they didn't really see it as that much of a holiday; more of a survival course. At the time I thought they enjoyed it as much as I did.

We maintained this routine from when they were five or six years old to early teenage, when they rebelled and refused to go any more, saying they'd had enough of sleeping rough, birdwatching in the clouds, looking for badgers and snakes, and trudging across hill and dale with a backpack and their wildlifer's kit of binoculars, microscope, stick and flask of Bovril.

One year we decided to take a softer approach and instead of the Scottish highlands or the Lake District, we'd go to the New Forest – with a tent. My salary would never stretch to meals out so we always took a week's provisions in the van but, as a further sop to luxury, on the way I would treat us all to the finest breakfast any transport café could provide. This would be the full Monty, with eggs, bacon, sausages, beans, fried bread, the lot, and they certainly lapped it up. The problem arose when I came to pay and realised that I'd left my wallet at home.

The lady was quite nice about it. While the kids – Carter was about nine and Kate eleven – tried to hide under the table from sheer embarrassment, I showed my ID and promised faithfully to send the money as soon as we got home.

The next mistake I made was to tell them that camping was not allowed in the New Forest, and there were special men called Agisters who rode around on horseback like a sort of police force, so we would have to hide from them. These agisters are also called marksmen, I told them, which was not to do with firing rifles but just because they marked all the ponies' tails in a certain way to tell where they were from.

Carter got quite excited about this undercover camping but Kate had a rather po look to her. She was always the sensible one and my idea of a super holiday, already palling in the eyes of a near teenage girl, was not made any more attractive by it being illegal. She made her objections quite clear, along with her views on parental responsibility but, to her credit, did not demand to be taken home immediately. She helped put up the tent in what I believed was a quiet spot, and we spent the last knockings of the day thoroughly enjoying ourselves, looking for adders and grass snakes.

We crept into our tent – a good, well made two-man ridge tent – and fell asleep, to be awoken at about three in the morning by the most tremendous, inexplicable noises. It sounded as though we were in the middle of our very own private cyclone. The tent was being buffeted and ripped, with lots of accompaniment from heavy breathing and different sorts of thud. I scrabbled around for the torch, crawled half out of the tent, and was confronted by a pair of large eyes. I knew there were no bears in the New Forest; what was I so worried about?

The animal backed away from the torch and tried to make off. It almost succeeded, but was held by the tangle of guy ropes and shreds of fabric that had recently been our tent, and which it had now lifted in its entirety from those sheltering within.

So, we spent the next hour in the dark, gradually untangling a New Forest pony from the remnants of our holiday home. Once free, it hurtled away without a word, and left us sitting, wrapped up in what we could salvage, awaiting the dawn. We didn't have long to wait but unfortunately it was signalled by thunder, lightning and a downpour of tropical proportions. We had our waterproofs, and a few bits of tent, so we didn't get quite as wet, cold and miserable as we might have, but my jokes fell rather flat about how lucky we were to be having these interesting experiences when we could have been like normal people, in a nice warm bed in a boring old Filey boarding house.

Come morning, the rain cleared away, the sun shone, and with renewed spirits we set forth to explore. We came across a very pretty stream, nine or ten feet wide, with steep banks and a fast flow of water. I said if we sat there a while, we'd be sure to see something. The kids were well trained in this sort of waiting, without fidgeting or making noises and so we sat in the sun, listening to the birds in the trees, when a flash of electric blue went past.

This is usually it when you see a kingfisher. You know you've seen it, because you saw the blue flash at high speed in level flight, at a precise height above the water, but you didn't really see a bird. I was a little surprised, because kingfishers prefer slow moving or still water, so I assumed that our little river was in something of a flood after the thunderstorm and would normally be more gentle.

I suggested looking for the nest. Kingfisher territories

are rarely more than a mile on a river so we should be able to find it, and we did. The tunnel was about halfway up the river bank, too high to see into it from below, and too far down, four feet or more, to see from above. Not that I should have expected to see much anyway, as the tunnels can be six feet long, lined with smelly fish bones and bird muck made of reconstituted fish. Kingfishers are not very houseproud.

I tried to get a look in but it was impossible, so I said I'd lower the children over the bank, holding on to their legs, so they could maybe see something even if I couldn't. Kate was having none of it and, muttering something about having a mad idiot as a father, stalked off and sat under a tree, arms folded and face set in disapproval.

Carter was just the opposite, very excited, desperately keen, and so I lowered him over the edge. I did have one reservation, hoping that the kingfisher would not decide to fly out just now, right into Carter's face, with accompanying criticism from Kate plus her full description to Carol about how her brother had got two black eyes and a puncture wound.

We'd slightly underestimated the distance from bank top to tunnel, and Carter kept saying, 'A bit further, Dad, a bit more, nearly there,' then he didn't say anything because he was in the river and I was lying flat out on the bank with a small blue wellington boot in each hand. I wasn't too concerned – the boy was a good swimmer – but the water was flowing fast and he was being swept away.

'That's it, that's it,' Kate screamed at me. 'Ruined our so-called holiday and drowned my brother!' But I was on my way. Crashing through the undergrowth I wasn't making any ground at all on my disappearing son, then the river took a bend away and back and I could cross the neck of it and get in the water ready to snatch him up as he came by.

He was okay, not frightened but, obviously, soaked to the skin. We hadn't brought much in the way of spare clothes because – as Kate was quick to point out – I'd said there wasn't enough room in the van, and by the time we got back to our campsite the boy was shivering, teeth chattering, gooseflesh all over. We stripped him off, towelled him, wrapped him in what we could – my jacket, Kate's jumper – and I set about lighting a fire. Kate went off in search of wood and, after too long, we had a good fire going with Carter's clothes drying around it on sticks.

They were steaming away well when the Agister turned up on horseback. He did not mince his words as he told me about the regulations concerning camping and lighting fires, and was launching into the general principles of parental duty of care when I interrupted him. The lad had fallen in the river while trying to catch minnows, and we weren't camping. We were only here for the day and we'd be moving on as soon as we could.

Kate said nothing. Her face told of a thousand silent words, many of which I suspected were being stored ready for recounting to Carol when we reached home.

13

RESCUING THE RESCUER

Covering for other inspectors – on holiday, off sick or temporarily not at post – was part of normal life, and it did sometimes mean operating in parts of Yorkshire that I otherwise wouldn't go to. One such territory went into a coalmining area, and an emergency call had me racing to the scene as fast as I could.

I happened to be in the local animal home when the call came in, not far away, and Beryl, the home's manager, came with me. There were some puzzling elements about the message, which said that a dog was stuck in some tarry stuff and was slowly sinking. Why, we asked each other as we drove, did someone not pull it out? Why did the caller just describe the scene and not do anything about it?

Through the village, past the colliery now working again after the miners' strike, we came to what you might call industrial archaeology, ramshackle buildings half fallen down, rusting ancient machinery and the remnants, we assumed, of some old part of the enterprise no longer in use. Part of the leftovers was a big trough, an open metal tank about the size of a cricket pitch, full of filthy-looking black sludge and, standing in the sludge, whimpering in fear and pain, was a black and white dog, a collie cross of some kind, and it was up to its stomach in this muck.

What Beryl and I couldn't understand was why there were three blokes watching it, showing some concern but not making any move to help the poor animal.

'What's up with you lot?' I said. 'Are you going to stand there?'

'Sorry, pal,' said one. 'Nobody's going to get mixed up with that stuff. Burn worse than fire, that will.'

'Caustic waste, mate,' said another. 'That's what they call it. Nowt to be made from it, no good for owt, and they won't pay to get rid, so it gets left.'

'But what about the dog?' I said.

'Aye, I know. Another pit accident.'

The animal was about four feet from the edge of this trough and obviously most thoroughly stuck and, equally obviously, in great pain and desperate need of rescue. In my anxiety I didn't connect what the men had said with the suffering of the dog, far more than being unable to move. In fact it was being burned alive but all I could think about was somehow getting it out of there.

I couldn't see my grasper being any use so I had to try to get hold of it myself. Leaning over I could just reach it but not get a proper grip, and its fur and skin came away in my hand. Beryl was trying to help too but not getting anywhere and the dog was no nearer, still sinking and utterly consumed by pain, which it was bearing in that stoical way that dogs have, and which brings tears to my eyes as I write this.

At last I realised what was happening, bloody fool that I was. There was no possibility of euthanasia by correct method, which was to inject pentobarbitone sodium into a vein, as there was no way of reaching a vein in these circumstances, much less raising same for the needle. The other way is intraperitoneal injection, which is a straight jab into the body cavity. This method is not so instantaneous as vein injection but I tried to counteract that by giving the dog maybe three times the approved dose.

We watched the dog die – quickly, thank goodness – and that was that. Nothing to be gained by trying to retrieve the body, especially as we were now finding out why the last half-hour of its life had been so miserable, and why the three blokes had refused to help. Our arms and hands were coming up in blisters, the skin red and peeling, the sensation, as the man said, like burning in fire.

We ran to the van, where there was always a tub of water, and gave ourselves a shower. On a hot day I only had a short-sleeved shirt and Beryl a thin blouse, which had protected us to an extent but would not be requiring laundering any more.

We drove to the colliery office and told them to get that tank covered over and sealed before some child fell into it and, gently nursing our blisters, went back to normal work.

Somebody must have been impressed because the local paper ran the story, which came to the notice of the great powers above, who gave me and Beryl the RSPCA Bronze Medal – for 'Gallantry' rather than for thinking first and acting second.

Well, I make no apologies for that. It's always been animals before everything, and it's an attitude that has got me into trouble occasionally. Or often, Carol might say.

Dog in caustic tank was a one-off, thank the Lord, but dog underground was a frequent occurrence and, usually, a heart-sinker because the outcome was rarely a success. Small dogs will get themselves into badger setts, fox earths and any other hole big enough. They get stuck, they can't turn round, they catch their collar on a root, they panic, they go further in, and we end up being able to do nothing. If we do try to dig them out, there is always the real danger of tunnels collapsing, burying the dog alive. Probably the worst places of all are old quarries, where rock falls are the danger and digging is the hardest work.

Four o'clock in the morning, phone rang, woman in tears, distraught with worry, her dog lost down a hole in a quarry. If that was the case, I thought as I got dressed and drove to her house as the sun came up, how did she know where it was, and why at four o'clock?

She was standing at her door when I arrived, face red with weeping, and insisted on taking me right away to the place. There was a field beyond her back garden, and beyond that a limestone quarry, not a big one and, from the amount of trees and other vegetation growing there, long since disused. She'd been following the dog, she said, and had seen it go in that hole, there, yesterday afternoon.

'Following it?' I asked.

'Yes,' she said. 'I had to, she wouldn't take any notice of me, just kept going.'

A cup of tea was in order and she could tell me the whole tale. The dog – see photographs all along the mantelpiece of a rather podgy Jack Russell bitch – was prone to phantom pregnancies and had been known to go off looking for a secret place to have the non-existent pups. This latest occasion had been much worse than before, with the dog digging up the carpet, pulling tea-towels off the kitchen rail and dragging the woman's smalls from the laundry basket into corners to make a bed. She'd taken her to the vet but that hadn't done any good; then yesterday she'd happened to look out of the window as little Mavis (Mavis? Oh well. Makes a change from Buster) finished digging a tunnel under the garden fence and disappeared.

She'd run after her, calling, but she paid no attention,

and she was just in time to see the dog go down the hole. Pleading with Mavis over and over again to come out, she'd sat by the hole until dark. Then she couldn't sleep for worry and, well, that was that.

I explained that the best thing to do was to wait forty-eight hours. There were two reasons for this. The dog might come out of its own accord, and I couldn't expect any help from the fire brigade until forty-eight hours had gone by. That was their rule. Cats up trees, dogs down holes, forty-eight hours before they'd turn out. I wanted the brigade, not because I expected them to quarry limestone for me, not yet anyway, but because they were the ones who had an endoscope among their kit – very expensive technology in those days, widely available at low cost now – and we in the RSPCA did not. With an endoscope, you can search down a hole and see what's happening, or not, through the video link.

This lady didn't seem all that impressed by my advice. I decided against saying that two days down a hole without food might slim Mavis down and make her escape that bit easier.

The problem in such cases was to try to persuade the owner that waiting was the best thing. The owner wanted action, and we had very little in the way of answers. Priority of course was to get some idea of where the dog was, but even if you could hear her barking or whining, sound travelling underground through tunnels and holes could never give you an accurate position. The iron rods and stethoscope I used when trying to find Her Ladyship's Westie were only any good in soft ground for a few feet down, so they were useless here.

Next morning, we sat by the hole for two hours and heard nothing. I had the woman's word that this was the right hole but I really needed some confirmation. With much else to do, I left her at her post, asking her to make a note of what, when and if she heard anything, and I'd be back later.

By mid-afternoon there were three messages from her, saying she'd heard the dog and would I come quick and, when I did get there, I too heard a very unhappy little whine but nothing like enough noise to permit an educated guess at how far in the dog might be.

Once more I explained that we had to wait, and I'd be back in the morning. She rang later, offering me any amount of money and telling me she'd heard Mavis barking. No money, thank you, although you can always make a donation to the RSPCA, and I'll be there first thing, I said, with a colleague to help. She started to turn nasty, saying I was incompetent and didn't care, and she was going to get the press on to it. I could hear her husband telling her to calm down, and he took the phone to say he'd the day off work so would be there to help us on the morrow.

The best thing always is to dig down towards the place you think the dog might be. In a limestone quarry this was not an option, nor was there a good spot to get a mechanical digger in – these are dangerous things anyway, increasing the likelihood of a rockfall.

Our only mode of attack was to follow the dog into the hole, making it bigger, hoping that we'd reach the animal before the going got too tough. My pal and neighbouring RSPCA inspector Dan turned up with pick and shovel and, with husband, we set to. Two hours' hard labour got us four yards.

A week and a day was my record for a dog rescue, when we moved enough earth to make a Stone Age burial mound. This time, I was fairly confident, it could not take as long as that before we won or lost, and by the time we stopped for our lunch break, we'd made another four yards. Now we could all hear the dog quite clearly and, we thought, not very far away. Perhaps we could get a sight of Mavis if we crawled into the tunnel with a torch. I say 'we', but it was me down the hole while Dan shouted encouragement and gave me helpful hints his grandfather had given him about digging coal in a confined space.

His singing the tune from *The Great Escape* didn't improve matters either, because that was exactly how I felt, trying to move along a tunnel too small for me, peering through the darkness with a small head-torch, and passing any loose bits of rock backwards. Every so often I stopped to listen, and I could hear Mavis and call her name, knowing that she'd hear me.

Two things happened at once. I got stuck, wedged in by

my shoulders, and the general cloud of dust in my torch beam turned into a shower.

I tried to push myself back but couldn't move. The shower of dust became a downpour, with small stones and earth mixed in. I shouted for Dan but my voice was lost in the storm. Not for the first time, I knew that an animal rescue was going to do for me. In my panic, all I could think about was what Carol would be saying at this moment, telling me what an idiot I was to risk everything for a fat little Jack Russell.

As the fall became more insistent, somehow my struggles worked and I wriggled back, to freedom I thought, but I was stuck again. This time Dan heard me and got far enough in to grab hold of one leg. The rocks and earth were hitting me hard, and if I wasn't a difficult enough job on my own to be pulled backwards by one leg, the extra weight of all the stuff on top of me made it harder still.

Dan, great friend that he was, got me far enough for the husband to grab the other leg, and together they retrieved a shaking, half-suffocated RSPCA man from the small avalanche that now blocked up the tunnel.

Over a cup of tea back at the house, I started burbling about getting a mechanical digger tomorrow but I was told to shut up and go home by Dan. He would take over now.

Carol and I had just finished our supper when the phone rang. It was the woman, crying again but this time tears of joy. Our avalanche must have opened up a route elsewhere and Mavis had come out, trotted home, and barked at the door to be let in as if nothing had happened.

14

WHERE FERRETS
FEAR TO TREAD

I must emphasise, and I cannot stress this enough, that the following story has nothing whatever to do with the UK National Ferret Welfare Society, nor any of its members or affiliated groups. Nothing in the story is connected with any of the many current ferret rescues and sanctuaries – in fact, the whole episode is entirely separate, distant and distinct from anything at all to do with anyone respectably associated with ferrets.

It all happened before the NFWS was founded, and before there were any ferret rescuers – in Yorkshire at any rate – and it was this very lack that started me off. I'd been a ferret fan since youth, when I first kept one, and I'd studied them a little. They are a variety of polecat, bred over the years for rabbiting and ratting but a polecat nonetheless, *Putorius foetidus*. Both of those words mean stinking, and our word ferret comes from a Latin word for thief, so you can't say ferrets have had a very promising classification.

Other people may worry about them being smelly, and their inclination to bite, but there's no such thing as the perfect friendship. What I worried about, as an RSPCA inspector, was the rotten care that most ferrets seemed to get. Far and away their main reason for being kept was to hunt rabbits, yet almost everyone I came across was feeding his (and it was almost exclusively men and boys) ferrets on bread and milk, and usually the standard white sliced bread, nutritionally valueless to polecats. No one seemed to make the connection between the ferret's instinct to pursue rabbits and the rabbit's instinct to run in terror, with the possibility of some raw meat in the ferret's feed dish.

It needn't be much, or expensive. Ferrets don't eat large amounts. They eat little and often. What about a bit of ox liver? Any kind of raw meat would have done. Or hard-boiled egg, pieces of chicken carcass from Sunday lunch, that sliced-off steak fat that someone left on the plate, that cold lump of yesterday's pork crackling that nobody wants – all fit in with the high-protein, high-fat, low-fibre intake that's natural to ferrets. You can get proprietary ferret food now. You couldn't then.

Apart from general poor health, one consequence of the white sliced diet was loose bowels. Ferrets are very clean animals. Their ancestral wild polecats will not defecate anywhere near where they live, and ferrets on a proper regime in a spacious cage will do the next best thing, which is to keep a small corner for a latrine. Bread and milk made ferrets scour, tidiness was not possible, and many owners came to accept a filthy cage as the normal thing.

Then having fed their animals on the most inappropriate grub, owners would expect them to be fighting fit, ready to dive down any hole or, much worse, to go ratting. Here the deal often was for the ferret to scare the rat into open ground – say, the floor of a barn – where a terrier would pounce and kill it. Some rats, however, would not run, and a big rat standing its ground against a vegetarian ferret may well come out on top.

My RSPCA phone never rang about a ferret but, out on other business, I knew if there was a ferret nearby. *Putorius foetidus* has a pretty powerful smell anyway; when being kept in the usual bad way, the smell reached across and called me. I'd sometimes just deliver a lecture and, sometimes, the owner was grateful. He'd had no idea he was doing anything wrong, just following everybody else.

Sometimes again, I'd end up taking the ferret away, which could make life very difficult. Other wild animals in my little zoo and care home didn't always take kindly to having a fiery polecat among them, and nobody at that time seemed to keep ferrets purely as pets, so a small ad in the classifieds seldom produced the desired result.

I tried to do something about this situation but, with no real resources, my drop in the ocean was a batch of leaflets, under the rather grand heading of The North Yorkshire Ferret Welfare Society, of which I was chairman, hon sec, treasurer and membership. The leaflets outlined a proper diet, cleaning routine and so on, and I handed them out at every opportunity. Quite how this came to the notice of two men from Huddersfield I don't know, but they wanted to talk to me with a view, they said, to setting up an all-Yorkshire Society for the Protection of Ferrets.

We met at a service station on the M62. I'm not sure what I was expecting but it certainly wasn't these two. One was Frank, who looked exactly like Benny Hill's character Fred Scuttle, with the milk-bottle-bottom glasses, and he talked like him too except with a broad West Yorkshire accent. The other was introduced by his nickname, Yogi, and looked like a half-Mexican version of Lee Van Cleef, with droopy moustache and long straggly hair. He had that mean kind of look that could have got him a part in any spaghetti western, as long as he didn't have to say anything because he too was as Huddersfield as they come.

In modern times, you might expect such fellows to dress in combat fatigues, with a US general's baseball cap, travelling in a giant black 4WD pick-up called something like Toyota Exterminator, with smoked windows and a great array of lamps rigged across the top. Back then, it was more army-surplus anorak, flat 'at and old Land-Rover.

I felt a little in awe of them. I was a young, idealistic RSPCA do-gooder, while they came across as real country characters, dyed in the wool, here when the grass grew, part-of-the-landscape Yorkshire.

That they were genuine ferret enthusiasts was not in doubt and, at the time, I couldn't see any further than that. They wanted me to be chairman of this great pan-Yorkshire organisation they were going to set up, and I should have asked more about what they thought I was bringing to the party. With hindsight, it's apparent that ferret welfare was important but it wasn't as important as getting rabbits to sell at a quid each. With the RSPCA link in a formal, official Society with a capital S, they were hoping that such additional respectability would gain them more and better rabbiting access to private land. And that, as we shall see, wasn't even the half of it. Yogi may well have been smarter than the average bear; he was certainly smarter than the average RSPCA inspector.

The first meeting of the new society was arranged, and it was to be held at a house in a village way up in the Pennines on a Sunday afternoon. It was a very nice house too, detached, good old Yorkshire stone, owned by a friend of Yogi's, with a large upstairs room that had a bar in the corner. I took my cousin Gary with me and we were a bit late, so there were maybe twenty men in there when we arrived, all apparently members in favour of the protection of ferrets.

Frank had put an agenda together, with various formal

matters to be resolved – badges, subscriptions, rules, election to committee and whatnot – that he rattled through in short order, which was just as well because of the beer. The house owner was a brewing hobbyist and he was selling his latest concoction, that he called Ferret's Breath, at ten pence a pint. It went down far too easily and then came back at you with a bang. It was a dark brew, something like Theakston's Old Peculier only stronger, and little organised thought could have been given by the chairman or the members to any agenda matters after the first hour.

Next came the fund raising. It was a bit like a garage sale. Members had scoured their lofts for unwanted items, and these were to be sold at knock-down prices to raise money for the cause. In our befuddled state, neither Gary nor I questioned why the items were unwanted. There were clocks, trousers, shirts, radios, a chainsaw, power tools, four Scalextric sets in their boxes, two professional-quality food mixers – nor did we ask why most of them came from one source, to be bought up eagerly by the others.

The source was a quite spectacular, villainous-looking fellow whom we immediately but secretly nicknamed Fagin. He wasn't tall but he had the hair and the features, including the worst set of teeth any dentist had never seen. Well, everybody was getting stuck into the Ferret's Breath and the rest of the meeting is a bit of a blur in my memory, and it was no use me asking Gary because he also can't remember how we came to be asleep in the car until dawn the next day.

Motorway services were the only places open so we stopped there for some breakfast and, gradually, the mists began to clear.

'Funny thing, that,' said Gary.

'Funny?' said I.

'Yes, all that stuff. Most of it new. Some of it still in the original packaging. Good quality, a lot of it.'

'And most of it coming from Fagin,' I said as a penny dropped somewhere with a loud ping.

We decided to go to one more meeting, to see for ourselves if, on the one hand, this had been a supremely generous gesture by one individual ferret fan to mark the foundation of the Society or, on the other hand, there had been a very different kind of ferreting going on and our members, as well as being everyday country folk, were also leading figures in the Huddersfield and West Riding Brotherhood of Fences, Receivers and Sellers-on.

Always expect the unexpected. Fagin wasn't at the next meeting so the garage sale was much more low key, although still with a suspiciously large proportion of new goods, and Yogi had a really special announcement to make. As Hon Sec of our Society, he had taken it upon himself to write to the Country Landowners' Association, offering to take a ferreting stand at the National Game Fair. This Game Fair I knew was absolutely the event of the year in field sports, held at a different country estate each time, such as Harewood House, Belvoir Castle or Ragley Hall. The country house where the next fair was to be held was not one of those.

Everyone was hugely enthusiastic about this fantastic opportunity to raise the image of ferret-keeping and spread the word of welfare, and many more pints of a new brew, called Goodnight Eddie Waring, were sunk in congratulations. Then Fagin turned up with a small velvet bag. He tipped out the contents – diamond rings, pearl necklaces, sapphire brooches – and said his auntie had died and left him this jewellery which, as it hadn't cost him anything, he would like to sell and donate the proceeds.

On the way home, Gary and I decided we would quietly retire from society activities, but would give the game fair a go as our last hurrah. The main reason for this lack of immediate effect was a condition of the offer. As we were to be at the show for the first time, our chairman, in his other persona as RSPCA inspector, was to go well in advance to meet the man in charge, at the country house, for a short interview of authentication. I went, met an imposing chap who had that pre-war, aristocratic accent you rarely hear these days, and told him about the objectives of the Yorkshire Society for the Protection of Ferrets as laid down in our constitution. He was quite satisfied with that, and in his turn gave me a brief address on the traditions of the game fair and the high standards expected of exhibitors.

Came the day before the weekend, we assembled at

Yogi's mate's place. Yogi had got hold of a minibus, which was not exactly in showroom condition. Apparently we would need to stop several times for petrol, not because of excessive consumption but because the rust had got through the petrol tank so it could only be filled to halfway. Fagin was there, and Frank, so we had The Three Effs plus about ten others from the twilight zone, and we set off as if on a rugby tour. Beer and whisky were being passed round before we'd gone ten yards, and there was no limit to the supply.

Thankfully the driver remained sober, or enough at least to understand the gateman's directions to the exhibitors' area, which was down a long driveway lined on either side by poles holding fancy white rope. None of your plastic tape rubbish here, obviously.

Next came the erection of tents. Alas, there was no such thing as a smartphone on which to film the scenes of chaos, for surely it was the sort of universal slapstick comedy that goes viral on YouTube. Even better would have been a silent film – a dozen and more drunken blokes, lurching around trying to put up tents they'd never seen before. Keystone Kops, eat your heart out.

Eventually, people crawled into half-erected tents for a late-afternoon nap, ready for the night out. There was a town not far away, sufficiently advanced in those non-cosmopolitan days to have both an Indian and a Chinese restaurant. The vote was for the curry house, despite knowing that we were sleeping close together in tents, and the pub crawl began. They had closing time in that far off puritan age, so we were forced by lack of beer out of the last pub at about a quarter to eleven.

Indian restaurants have always expected an influx at chucking-out time, but they weren't so culinarily sophisticated then, and neither were their customers. Curries were judged on how hot they were, so our mob went for the Madras, Vindaloo and Bangalore Phall end of the menu.

I can't remember if we were thrown out of the restaurant because it was closing or because we were drunk and disorderly. A contributory factor may have been Fagin, so drunk that he fell asleep in his Bangalore Meat Special, the out-breaths from his snores sending pilau rice and pieces of chilli across the table. Anyway, we set off again in the minibus, stopping a couple of times for people to have a jimmy riddle or be sick, but that hardly interrupted the jollity with which the driver was joining in, singing 'On Ilkley Moor Baht 'at' with as much gusto as the rest.

We had a pass to get in the exhibitors' gate but there was no one there when we turned up well after midnight. I was sitting at the back, not exactly as sober as a judge but sober enough to wonder why, as we went down the long driveway, the bus was veering from side to side, like a yacht tacking, to the accompaniment of laughs and cheers. There were also some bumps and clattering noises, the cause becoming obvious when we stopped and got out, about fifty yards short of our encampment.

The bus was gaily and profusely decorated with white rope, festooned even, as we had collected every item of temporary fencing on the way by clever use of the wing mirrors. We had the full length of it, with all the poles, right from the beginning, maybe a mile back, trailing behind us.

I made some half-hearted suggestions about putting it all back but nobody took any notice. Fagin, refreshed by his Bangalore snooze, pulled out a foot-long Bowie type knife and slashed the ropes free. Home James, he said, and nobody will know it was us.

Oh yes they will, I thought, wondering if Gary and I should start walking home now. Gary said we'd get up very early and disappear before the storm broke, so that became our plan. What seemed like minutes later, I heard my name being called.

'Inspector Langdale. Would you care to account for this?'

'This' was Frank, held by his collar by one of the three stewards who stood outside my tent, dressed in tweed Norfolk jacket and plus-fours, knitted stockings with a red ribbon, and finely polished brogues. Frank looked as if he'd been pulled backwards through a bramble patch.

'Is this man with you?' said the steward holding him, while the other two showed me what they were carrying: about a dozen each of rabbits and pheasants.

'Honest, Mr Langdale, I was just out for a walk and I found them, and I was bringing them back to ask you what to do,' said Frank.

The others were spilling out of the tents, and a right motley crowd they were. The stewards looked at them with a mixture of disgust and disbelief, and at the long trail of destruction that had been their exhibitors' driveway. They had no proof of any misdemeanour and, examining the potential witnesses, decided they would never get any.

'You have fifteen minutes to decamp. If you are not on your way by that time, we'll call the police. Now, get moving, and you can be sure that the Yorkshire Ferrets Club, or whatever you call yourselves, will be forbidden entry to every field sports event in this country, *sine die*.'

'Carter, what's it mean, syni deeay?' asked Gary later.

'It's Latin. They use it in court. It means never, ever again, no matter how long you live.'

15

GOING OVER THE EDGE

Always keen to explore the outer limits, I trained in abseiling and rope rescue to become one of the designated RSPCA men to be called on when an animal fell over the edge of a cliff or something similarly dangerous. Depending on who was available at the time, I could be sent to rescues miles away in the Peak District, up in the high Pennines, the Lake District or, in this case, at Flamborough Head.

This famous promontory, between the bays of Filey and Bridlington, has chalk cliffs up to 400 feet high that are much favoured by breeding seabirds, thousands and thousands and thousands of them. It has one of the two UK mainland gannet colonies, and gannets were the reason for the call.

They're migratory birds that don't breed until four or five years old, during which time they might join a different colony from their birth one but, once they have bred, they will return again and again to the same place and, if it's still there, the same nest. They lay only one egg (unless it is lost, when they'll lay a replacement), so there's just one chick and here lies a problem of the modern age.

It is father gannet's job to refurbish and maintain the nest which, on the gale-swept cliffs of Flamborough, is a more or less continuous task. Floating around in the sea, he will see bundles of nylon twine, bright blue or orange, that have come away from fishing nets and that look to him like perfect nesting material.

If there's too much of this stuff, out of balance with the natural components such as seaweed and other bits and pieces of vegetation, the chick can get tangled up in it. At eleven or twelve weeks old, the chick is meant to glide down to the sea, where it lives off its reserves while learning to fish and fly properly. Entwined in nylon mesh, it will be unable to leave the nest in due time, and will be left to die when its parents set off on the journey south.

Every winter, the coastguards used to combine with the RSPB and the RSPCA to mount a nest-cleaning exercise, abseiling down the cliffs below the village of Bempton, swinging on the end of a rope several hundred feet long, throwing dead gannet chicks into the sea and collecting all the nylon. Nobody could stop the male gannets gathering more next year but at least they would start with a clean nest.

Three long, stout metal pegs were driven into the ground with a sledgchammer, and the rope was threaded through to make your belay. To descend you had the standard figure-of-eight, which is a solid aluminium device with a small hole and a large hole through which you pass your rope and which allows you to run free or brake, depending on how you put on pressure.

For climbing back up, at the RSPCA we trained using the prusik method, having two loops of cord attached to your rope by prusik knots, which loosen when not under tension. You clip one loop to your chest harness and put a foot in the other. The knot tightens on the rope, you haul/push yourself up maybe eighteen inches, depending on how tall you are, lean down, pull the foot loop up, stand in it again to gain another eighteen inches, and so on. It's very tiring, especially when you have a rescued dog in your backpack.

The coastguards had a different method. A reduced tug-of-war team of three or four men took hold of your rope and marched away from the cliff edge, hauling you up rather more speedily but, if you were used to prusiking, it could seem like the white-knuckle rollercoaster ride you'd rather not go on.

Those cliffs are intimidating anyway, but in the winter, with the wind enough to bowl you over and the wild waves crashing so far below, it's quite sufficient to make the most experienced abseiler nervous. Just to add a little frisson, a telly crew was there that day – a typical grey Flamborough November day – to make a piece for a wildlife programme.

Another extra was Malcolm, a recently joined RSPCA inspector, still on probation as it were. The practice was to give the new boys as much experience as possible in their early days, so if there was anything especially interesting or unusual going on, management would send a Malcolm on detachment. I raised a query when contacted about this one, suggesting that abseiling down Bempton cliffs in winter wasn't exactly the stuff of induction courses, but no, Malcolm would be all right, he was ex-Army and fully trained in rope rescue.

He confirmed this himself when we met, but there were signs that perhaps we were not talking about the same thing when I described the coastguard hauling-up technique. Maybe I was imagining it but I thought he lost some of his natural colour, but no, he was sure he'd be able to handle that, so I went on to explain that I would go over first, so he could watch what I did, then he'd go over, and I would be at the top to make sure everything was tickety-boo.

Looking back, this all seems terribly wrong. I only had his word that his army experience left him up to the job in hand. Soldiers train by abseiling down viaducts, ready to mount a surprise attack on the village. Bempton cliffs in a freezing gale, with a three- or four-hundred-foot drop onto rocks and raging sea, was perhaps too much of a proposition.

Still, Malcolm said he could do it, and he repeated that after I'd shown him exactly where we would be working, peering over the cliff edge from one of the viewing points they had then. Those are the nests, right down there, I said – right down there being a good 250 feet or more.

Tourists look at this place in the summer, sunny day, still windy, always windy but not as windy, with cliffs covered with white gannets, puffins, fulmars, little auks, and the sea still crashing in but not as threatening when it's blue and white. Today, bleak November, overcast, sea black, cliffs naked, the occasional gale-tossed gull the only sign of life, the whole business had a much darker, more threatening edge to it, and Malcolm certainly felt it. He really did go pale this time, and rocked on his heels.

'You don't have to do this, Malcolm,' I said. 'You can just watch. You don't have to go over. Nobody's forcing you.'

I'd heard of people turning green, and Malcolm was on the way to that, his face a yellowish white with a hint of seasick, but no, he would do it all right. I thought back to my own time as a trainee. I was so desperate to do well that I'd have taken on any challenge they'd thrown at me. How lucky I was that they hadn't thrown this.

I was now a TV cameraman as well as everything else, with a very heavy so-called lightweight camera attached to my helmet like a large miner's lamp made of lead. I went over in standard fashion, walking backwards, abseiling down in gradual leaps, and spent half an hour clearing out nests until a combination of frostbite, windburn, hypothermia and delirious visions of hot coffee overcame my sense of duty and I radioed to be pulled up by the tug-of-war coastguards.

There could be no possibility of Malcolm wearing that camera so I checked anxiously that my amateur pictures had been okay. I took off my harness and handed it to Malcolm, who was shaking. I asked him again, and again during the age it took him to get the harness on, if he was sure about this.

I'd been a great Biggles fan as a boy, which had taken me on to reading about real flyers in the Great War, and one, the American Eddie Rickenbacker, said: 'Courage is doing things you're afraid to do. There is no courage without fear.' The question here was not that Malcolm was afraid to do it – that much was obvious – but rather whether he could overcome his fear.

I know now I should have stopped it there and then. I should never have allowed things to get this far. Disaster lurked over that cliff edge.

Although it's contrary to instinct, abseilers are trained to stand up straight and walk backwards over the edge and, when confidence is gained, they don't have a problem with that. Novices will always want to get nearer the ground, to bend knees and slither over, which may feel safer but in

174

fact is quite the opposite as it can lead to tangles and loss of control.

Malcolm, the experienced army abseiler, showed himself to be a rank beginner – either that or Bempton had made him forget everything he'd learned. He wriggled backwards on his hands and knees and stopped. A coastguard came to ask me if this was really a good idea. Still thinking Malcom should be given the chance to do the job and get a good report, I let it go to the next stage, with Malcolm over the edge but not yet disappeared as he 'abseiled' all of a yard.

At last, common sense prevailed and I gave the nod to the coastguards who pulled him back up. Still saying that he could have done it, and would have done it, and actually would still do it, the relief in Malcolm was apparent to all, as his face went from the grey it had recently become, back through white to normal.

I told him to go and get a hot cup of something, and thanked providence that he had not done the thing he was afraid to do.

*

Geoff, my senior boss in Sheffield, was even dafter than me, especially when it came to rescues. Having been a professional climber and mountain rescue guide before the RSPCA, he was top expert in that area and a great leader of men. The only problems were (1) he always wanted to do the rescue himself, and (2) he was a brusque, abrupt

Yorkie, intimidating perhaps, which meant that one or two people didn't get on with him.

I got on with him all right. He trained me in rope rescue and, as we got to know each other, he would tend to phone me first when there was something good on, by which we both meant something with an edge to it. Of course the animal to be rescued was always the point, but if the rescue was hard, tricky, dangerous or deeply uncomfortable, so much the better.

One Saturday morning in November, an off-duty weekend, Geoff was on the phone saying he wanted me to come on a rope rescue in the Peak District. I started to say that I was scheduled to paint the bathroom but that had no priority for Geoff (or me) over the attempted rescue of a kitten down a mine shaft in Derbyshire, and it was my turn to do the rescue.

We met at a village near Matlock, then had a trek of about forty-five minutes across the hills in the pouring rain, carrying all the ropes and rescue gear that Geoff always had ready in his van. The couple who had raised the alarm, who had 'heard a kitten mewing', were experienced rambler types (they'd have had to be, out in that filthy November weather), and had provided highly specific instructions, with map references, on how to reach the spot, with repeated assurances that they had indeed heard a kitten down a mine shaft in deepest Derbyshire. We reached the place in standard RSPCA winter clothing, which was the greatcoat. There was no super-waterproof, lightweight, breathable climbing kit; we had a big heavy woollen overcoat that got heavier and heavier as it got wetter.

Lead mining in that region finished many years ago and most of the old shafts have collapsed or been blocked or fenced off, but there are still some holes in the ground for the unwary to fall into. Quite how a kitten had fallen into one, in the middle of the White Peak miles from civilisation, we could not tell, but we knew what the challenge would be when we found it.

Here was a typical bell pit, a vertical narrow shaft about a yard wide with the spoil from digging it thrown around the entrance, so it looked like a miniature, flattened-out volcano. We could expect a wider chamber somewhere beneath, where they'd dug out the lead ore, although how far beneath we had no idea. As we looked down the black hole and listened, hearing nothing but the wind and the rain, Geoff said he would go. I said no he wouldn't, it was my turn, he'd done it last time, and so that was decided upon, although Geoff couldn't resist telling me about the poison gases that often lurked in these old mines. I didn't know if he was winding me up or what, but he told me to be very careful because these gases could not be detected before they overcame you. I asked him what would be the point of being careful, if care was going to make no difference. He just gave me an enigmatic look and said I had to keep in regular touch.

We had no radios or mobile phones, so communication was by shouting and rope-tugging – one tug for I'm okay, two tugs and I'm coming back up, three tugs for send down a cat basket. We also tied a knot ten feet up from the bottom of the 300 feet rope, so that I'd know I was just ten feet from falling off the end.

I'd descended nowhere near that far when the shaft narrowed and I was stuck. Geoff lowered a folding spade down to me, the sort soldiers carried in World War One for digging trenches, and I bashed away at the limestone with that. The rain was still reaching me as I swung on my rope, held by the figure-of-eight, trying to see what I was doing with an ordinary torch (no headtorches then).

During the hour it took me to widen the shaft enough to find a way through, Geoff must have asked me a dozen times if I wanted him to take over, and I wasn't very far off saying something quite rude when a rock came away and I was abseiling again, into the unknown. The torch showed only a little bit of the shaft sides but nothing of what lay below. Anyway, when I was on the move I needed two hands so the only way I could hold the torch was in my armpit, which didn't help much.

I was sniffing the air for Geoff's poison gases, meanwhile realising that if I failed to sniff in time and lost consciousness and therefore my grip, the figure-of-eight wouldn't hold and I'd be gone. Such thoughts lend that edge to the excitement that I mentioned earlier.

It took me another half an hour to reach the bottom, a

small chamber with two passages running off. I reckoned I'd come about 70 feet and wondered if a kitten could survive such a fall and, if it had, whether it had gone on down the smaller of the two entries, about eighteen inches high, which would have meant the end of any rescue attempt.

On my knees I listened. Nothing. I turned the torch off and listened again in the blackness, that deep, deep blackness you only get underground, where no light penetrates.

With no clue on kitty, my only option was to explore the larger of the two passages, which was about a yard in diameter – about the same as the last time I was in a limestone tunnel, when it fell on my head. If that happened here, there was no Dan to pull me out.

Actually, there was another option, which was to leave a cat trap baited with food and hope the kitten would come to it. The implications of this – a daily visit to the mineshaft, a daily abseil down to the trap and a return tramp across the hills – made it definitely second best as a choice.

I wriggled through the tunnel for a few yards without too much trouble, calling, 'Puss, puss,' and getting no reply, but the job was getting harder and the torch was becoming less useful in penetrating the clouds of dust I was making in the blackness. And then, the moment. I heard it. I heard a weak, pathetic, tiny mew and I knew my living had not been in vain.

A few more feet and I could see cat's eyes in the torchlight. Now, the worry was if it would take fright and run. There was no possibility of my following it for any distance. Stay there, puss, stay there, please stay there.

The more I called, the more response I had, and then I saw it properly, a miserable, terrified little waif, black and white, maybe twelve weeks old. I reached towards it, where it crouched in a crevice in the rock, and stroked its head. The mew changed to a purr and I knew I was home. I grabbed it by the scruff and pulled it towards me. Claws were instinctively out but it didn't try to bite as a feral cat would have done, so I stuffed it down the front of my greatcoat and began my reverse wriggling. If my nose and throat hadn't been full of dust I'd have broken into song.

In the chamber, large enough to sit upright if not to stand, I could retrieve the purring little beastie and examine it. The poor thing was an absolute bag of bones and very dehydrated. You test this by pinching the skin on the back of the neck. Normally it would return to normal when you let go, but the skin of a dehydrated animal stays where it is.

I shouted up to Geoff to find some water from somewhere, collect the rain if need be, while I prussicked back up. Tired as I was, the adrenalin was flowing and I was up there in no time. We had no food with us but the kitten lapped up the water, and the journey back to the vans with it in my coat seemed to fly by. There we had some tins of fish recipe, but we only fed a little. You can't give a starving animal loads of food; that's asking for trouble. So, cruel to be kind, we watched the little kit eat its spoonful of food in half a second, put it in a basket and said our goodbyes, still with no idea about how such a small domestic animal could end up in a mineshaft so far from any possibility of home.

Geoff, the great instigator of rescues that many others would never contemplate, pointed out that it was his turn next, and I could only hope that it would prove every bit as interesting as my turn had been.

I took the kitten home, fed it some more and, over the next weeks, watched him fill out and regain full health. After fourteen years as Marbles the Mystery Cat, our family cat, he did what cats so often do. Without making a fuss, he disappeared away somewhere to die in peace.

16

ALL CREATURES GREAT AND SMALL

Vets are enormously important to an RSPCA inspector who, if he's new on the job, will tend to take them as they come, respect their words and opinions, and not argue. This was especially so when I started and picked up the name of a veterinary practice in Scorswick that had its surgery on one of the main streets, right opposite a cinema.

I say 'surgery' – really it was more of a time warp. The two vets, Mr McAllister and Mr McSweenie, known universally behind their backs as Haggis and Co., had trained just after the war, or maybe during it, had set up their business in the likeness of the ones they'd trained in, and hadn't changed it since. There was no modern equipment – nothing newer than 1955; their one concession to progress was an X-ray machine but even that was probably driven by clockwork.

They didn't stock any modern drugs. They knew about antibiotics and suchlike of course, but if something like that was required for an animal patient, they would write out a prescription and the client – in some cases me – would get it from the high street pharmacy and, naturally, pay for it. This I am sure was a unique arrangement. I've never heard of anything like it since.

Otherwise they relied on the old remedies, and would make them up in the back room from a most impressive array of bottles and jars containing lurid liquids with labels displaying abbreviated Latin names, also the contents of a mysterious wooden dresser with a hundred little drawers, wherein were kept powders and, for all I knew, eye of newt and toe of frog. There were jars of whale fat that they used to make ointments, and PULV. of this, EXTR. of that and AQ. of the other. Compared to this, James Herriot's surgery was the last word in advanced technology.

That their remedies worked I could not doubt. I had a semi-sprained ankle once, greatly swollen, and Mr McAllister told me to wait a minute. He emerged from the back room with a bottle of grey water. 'Lead and opium,' he said. 'Pour it on, soak your sock in it.' So I did, and the swelling went down almost before my eyes.

The common view that Scotsmen are tight with money is, I am sure, largely a myth and a vile calumny, but there must be a germ of truth in it somewhere if Haggis and Co.

were anything to go by. Their thriftiness with the tools of their trade was matched by their satisfaction on receipt of the fees coming their way when they appeared in court as my expert witnesses. This regular and highly nutritious addition to their practice income had no effect whatever on the fees they charged me and the RSPCA.

They didn't have a proper operating theatre, although they had a room where they did operations, and they were very reluctant to use it for the post mortems that were a fairly frequent reason for my visits. Establishing cause of death was critical to success in many cases of cruelty. Haggis and Co. were perfectly willing and competent, but they insisted on doing the post mortem in the back of my van, out in the street.

Usually we could get away with this, without causing too much of a stir, no thanks to Mr McAllister who took delight in embarrassing me, this new RSPCA boy, as much as he possibly could. On one occasion there had been a series of reported incidents of cats being shot with a .22 air rifle, but we had no witnesses until someone heard a shot, saw a young lad with a gun, and saw a ginger tomcat fall off a fence. It was now worth having a post mortem done on the cat. Maybe we could find the bullet, the lead slug, and link it to the gun in true forensic fashion.

Mr McAllister decided that the matter could be resolved only by skinning the cat, and his way of doing it was to make the necessary incisions, then hold the cat up by its back legs and pull the entire skin right off, past the head and away. He did this a little like the executioner holding up the head of Charles the First, waving it about for all to see, only his audience was the normal kind of innocent passers-by you generally had on a high street on a Saturday lunchtime.

*

Then I ran up against a certain Mr Pipe, known as Plumber for obvious reasons, who was to become a regular client of mine and a thoroughly unpleasant piece of work. He was an animal dealer. He may have started off in a reputable way, dealing in cattle and sheep, but his stock in trade now was quite different. He had several specialities, one of which was supplying dogs to a certain university laboratory for research. The university may well have believed the dogs were honestly got, but I knew they were strays or household pets on the wander, kidnapped by Plumber Pipe and sold on.

Another 'revenue stream' was all the clapped-out, broken-mouthed, dry-uddered sheep at the auction mart that nobody wanted. He'd buy them for almost nothing, slaughter them using his version of the halal system, and sell the meat (halal assured) to the less fussy end of the curry house business. He'd been to prison on two occasions that I knew about, and a visit to his so-called farm would be a regular thing.

On this day I found three goats and two sheep in dreadful condition. Two of the goats had broken legs, one of which was gangrenous, so I had to shoot them there and then. The other three animals were already dead, two sheep seemingly from starvation, the third goat from strangulation due to getting knotted up in its tether. I phoned Haggis and Co., got Mr McAllister, and was told to turn up a three o'clock.

He emerged from his premises, threading his way through the shoppers on the pavement, wearing his usual slaughterman's apron, a mighty construction of black rubbery material reaching from neck to floor and held in the middle with a length of bailer twine. He also had with him, in full view, his favourite knife for this work, another relic of the slaughterhouse, a long, wicked-looking thing that he kept sharp with the steel he also was never without.

As I said, we could get away with this procedure, even on a busy shopping afternoon – if it was one small dog or cat – but there were five large animals here in the back of my little Ford Escort van, and a couple of them had been dead for some time. Mr McAllister would be primarily concerned with the contents of the stomach, or lack thereof, and his incisions immediately caused an outflow of nauseous gases and a gradual drip of partially digested, miscellaneous vegetation in the form of a foul kind of slurry.

This, mixed with blood, was soon too much for the confines of the van and began to run down the street. People came to look. Children made horrified noises. I tried to keep them away. McAllister could not have cared less. He was oblivious. He made his notes on his little bloodstained pad while I pushed and swept sheep- and goat-guts back into the van.

He was a meticulous worker, slow and steady, and by the time he'd cut his way to the fifth animal there was a long queue forming outside the cinema. I've no idea what was on – *Dracula*, *House of Frankenstein*, *Don't Look Now* – but if it was blood and guts they were there to see, they could have saved their money with a brief spec inside my van.

This was my last post mortem with Haggis and Co. They had been very good to me, and I admired and liked them very much, but the image of the RSPCA was not being well served by roadside butchery on that scale. I had to go elsewhere and, soon afterwards, Messrs McAllister and McSweenie retired, doubtless well insulated against financial privation by the huge stack of court fees they'd earned and by their rigorous implementation of that old Caledonian proverb, 'Mony a mickle maks a muckle'.

17

MY ZOO AND
OTHER ANIMALS

There was never any room in our garage for the RSPCA van – not because it was like most garages everywhere, full of junk, tumble drier, DIY gear, holiday canoe, bicycles and whatnot, but because every square inch of wall and floor space was taken up with the cages, baskets and boxes of my private wildlife rescue centre.

The annexe was an aviary in the garden, where birds could convalesce from, say, a damaged wing, and regain their strength, before I could release them back into the wild. There were also various unofficial and temporary annexes, that is corners of rooms in the house, where animals rested that had to be kept nice and warm.

Spring was high season for this high-endeavour, high-reward (spiritual/ emotional), loss-making enterprise,

189

when young birds fell out of their nests and all wild animals became more active in the world, and so had more accidents and/or were more likely to be picked up unnecessarily by a well-meaning member of the public.

The activity was constant. Carol and I had no social life at this time of year. Every non-working moment was spent feeding, mucking out and treating just about every species in the book, morning, noon and night. Carol did most of the looking after of our two children as well. We were young and foolish. We just got on with it, mashing up worms to feed to baby birds, giving a baby hedgehog its breakfast milk with a syringe, and it was absolutely great.

Right from the beginning I'd spent lots of time at scientific gatherings and symposiums about wildlife rehabilitation. I'd read every learned article on the subject and talked to every expert I could find, so when spring came around I felt well prepared, for the usual and for the inevitable surprises that Mother Nature would throw at me every year.

An adult buzzard had a broken wing. The vet put a splint on it but it was going to be weeks, maybe months, before it was fit enough to go back into the wild. I didn't then know that raptors, and some other species such as parrots, imprint on the person caring for them. It's not like young geese who will follow you everywhere thinking you're their mother. This is sexual imprinting. Regardless of your own gender, the bird regards you as its mate and, as with our own species, various important attitudes come along with that relationship.

When the buzzard was well enough to be moved out of the garage my options were quite limited. Obviously a large bird of prey couldn't go in the aviary with the other birds, so I got hold of a bow perch and a few more falconry requisites. A bow perch is basically a steel semi-circular hoop with both ends in the ground. The perching bit has a thick covering, usually rubber, and the bird is on a short leash.

After a long time indoors, my buzzard needed to go through a process called weathering, aptly named because that's what happens. Some ill-informed people think that tethering a raptor for long periods on a perch is cruel, but that's what it does in the wild. It hunts, feeds, then snoozes on its perch for hours. So, I fed it, it went into its usual post-prandial, semi-somnolent state, then perched, busy doing nothing.

I should have noticed something odd one day when Carol was mowing the lawn while I was fiddling about in the aviary. The buzzard hadn't been out long and had not got around to any kind of proper flying. Generally it jumped off its perch, flapped around a bit, then hopped back on. This time, it was like a puppy dog on a leash, straining and pulling towards Carol as she moved up and down the garden.

My turn to mow the lawn next week, and I had daughter Katie with me on a beautiful sunny summer's day. Neither she nor Carter junior had any childish fear of strange animals, hardly surprisingly, and even something as big and rather special as an adult buzzard could not overawe my little nine-year-old.

She went right up to it and bent down to have a close look. It did something new. It flew straight up, into her face, and grabbed hold of her with its talons. Of course she screamed in terror, and of course I had the buzzard off her in seconds, but her face was lacerated. Luckily, the talons seemed to have missed her eyes and, by the time we'd cleaned her up and got her to A & E, she'd stopped crying and was being brave and calm.

The doctor gave me quite a lecture on professionalism as regards wild animals, health, safety and so on, which had Carol nodding in agreement. When all the coals had been hauled over, he announced that he would have to stitch Katie's eyelid. There was a small tear in the lower part of the lid, and he told Katie that it wouldn't hurt very much.

She nodded her agreement too, and the doc went to work. He'd been on the job five seconds when there was a loud thump behind us, as Carol hit the floor in a total faint. Doc had to leave Katie while he attended to Carol, who came round quite quickly, and brave daughter never flinched as he completed that part of the family treatment.

Carol was never one for opening old wounds or criticising those unfortunates who remember too late to shut the stable door, but this was her daughter who could have lost an eye and been disfigured for life. It was some time before the lamps of peace burned brightly again, without flickering.

During my wildlife high season, the first thing I did on coming home from the day's calls was check what was in the hallway. Anything brought in during the day would have been left there in a basket or cage by Carol, after receiving first aid as required, for me to decide what to do with it. I came home one day to find nothing in the hall but a very powerful smell in the air. It took me back to my childhood in Hull, the fish docks, the fish-meal factories – what was going on?

'Look in the bathroom,' came a shout from the kitchen, with an unspoken 'and get it sorted quick' added on the end. I looked as bidden, and saw a half-grown common seal having a cold bath. When seal pups are washed up on the shore, nine times out of ten they'll be washed back again and will find their mothers but people will pick them up and take them elsewhere, by which time it's too late to put them back where they were. Some kind person from the next village had been on a trip to the seaside and, finding it stranded on the sand, had brought this seal back in the car.

I went to the animal-food deep-freeze and took out some herrings.

'And where are you going with those?' said Carol.

'I'm going to feed the seal,' said I.

'No you're not,' said Carol. 'You're going to put that

animal in your van and you're going to drive it to the coast and put it back in the water. You can have your tea when you get back. I'll leave it in the oven when I go to bed.'

'I can't do that. It'll never find its mother now.'

'I'll be finding my mother very shortly, and her spare room.'

'Be reasonable, Carol. Look, it doesn't have to be in the bath.'

'I thought its skin had to be kept wet.'

'No, that's porpoises. It'll be all right in the garage.'

Obviously it was my fault that I hadn't told Carol in advance that seals didn't need to be kept in water. It lived in the garage in a large-size Vari Kennel (proprietary plastic kennel) for a month and more with the window open, and when it was fat and grown up enough I drove it to the nearest seaside and off it went.

Anyway, at least the bathroom was free for a while, until the great crested grebe arrived. These are fabulous birds, lake dwellers, with amazing plumage around their heads and necks that was a fatal attraction to Victorian ladies' bonnet makers, so much so that the bird almost became extinct in the UK until the RSPB was set up to protect it. Mine had a damaged wing, nothing too serious but it wouldn't be able to fly for a week or two. The problem I had was, it wouldn't eat. I had sild, whitebait, which it ignored when I dangled it, and still ignored when I put it in a bowl of water. I had to restort to force-feeding, which really wasn't very satisfactory, until I had an idea. What if my bird saw the fish while it was swimming? I mean, while the bird was swimming; I didn't have any live fish.

Without discussing my idea with my wife, I filled the bath, put some fish in the bottom, and gently placed my grebe on the water. At first it just paddled around, splashing its feathers, preening, doing what it would normally do on the lake, then it saw the fish. Down it dived, up it came, shook itself dry and swallowed the food. I was in ten kinds of delight, not only that the feeding problem had been solved, but because it had been my own genius of an idea that had solved it.

So pleased was I that I might have kept the bird longer than was strictly necessary, giving it two fish-baths a day, but fish, fowl and bathrooms do not mix in the eyes, minds and noses of mothers of small children, and I had to launch my great crested grebe back onto its home waters in the nature reserve.

18

HOW TO DROWN A SWAN

Rehabilitation of small birds is generally a simple matter. You just take your sparrow, robin, thrush, whatever, to a suitable spot and let it go. Without mother to show it, even the youngest ones have the necessary instincts for finding food. It's different with birds of prey. Fledglings brought to me would be used to having their food delivered and would not have had the chance to develop their hunting skills. They needed what we call a soft release.

The predator species I saw the most of was my boyhood friend, the tawny owl. The typical nest is in a hole in a tree, and where there are three chicks, often the case, things can get crowded. The parents feed the chicks for weeks after they're fledged so they get big and one might fall out. I'd have maybe a dozen or more young tawnies brought to me every season, and I had to devise a system especially for them. The two essentials were food and temporary accommodation. Food was not a problem; we had a hatchery near us where they bred laying hens for egg production. The practice was (and is) to sex the chicks at a day old and kill the males, which was done there by gas, and which gave me a steady and free supply of food for owls, snakes and other carnivores.

Accommodation also proved to be easy, as a friendly farmer was happy to install the young owls in a barn with an open window. I'd have already got them used to having chicks for dinner, so we could place one or two outside the window, on the ledge at first, then further away as the bird grew up into flying. The owl would go out for longer and longer periods, coming back to the barn every time, until it cottoned on to the notion of foraging for itself, becoming less and less dependent on the chicks we left, and set off to find its own territory and a mate.

'We' in this case was the farmer's daughter and me. She took a great interest in the process and had her reward when the owls came back to see her, and perched on her bedroom window sill in the morning when she got up for school.

The course of life for an RSPCA inspector never did run smooth, well, not mine anyway, but I had no suspicions when the phone rang and I was asked for my advice about the soft release of a young owl. The woman sounded very down to earth, no nonsense, was obviously a committed bird lover and experienced with other sorts of birds if not owls, so it was a bit of a shock when I met her. She asked me to call at her house to see the birds she had; I imagined a homemade aviary in a back garden.

I found the address, in a part of Scorswick I rarely visited where all the houses were large detacheds with long driveways. In this driveway was a top-of-the-range Mercedes convertible, and the lady who answered the door was exactly the glamorous, expensively dressed type you might expect to see driving such a car in designer shades and Hermes headscarf. She introduced herself as Linda, and took me to her aviary. Another shock.

It wasn't in the garden. It was in a very expansive and expensively fitted kitchen, with solid oak units all around the walls. She explained that she had only recently taken up bird rescue as an interest, and she hadn't known what to do with the first one she'd rescued, so she'd taken the door off one of the units and nailed a piece of chicken wire in its place. Over the previous summer, she'd done this to more and more units until her kitchen was full of birds making a terrific racket. The fridge and the cooker were still visible but I have no idea where she kept her pots and pans.

Although she could see the need for a proper aviary long term, she thought the current arrangements were fine for now and was happy to spend many hours every day feeding and mucking out, wearing clothes that would have cost my year's salary for one outfit. Naturally I wondered what her husband thought about it all, but he was a showbiz agent who spent a lot of time in London and, it seemed, his opinions didn't really count anyway.

Linda became my unpaid bird assistant. If there was a call to a bird in trouble and I couldn't get there quickly, I'd phone her and she would go in her Merc to pick it up, take it to the vet as necessary, and pay the bill. On a couple of occasions when my van was in for a service, she lent me the Merc as my duty vehicle, not minding at all how many mangy dogs or flea-ridden hedgehogs I had in the back. Of course it caused a few problems. There are people in certain parts of Yorkshire who will not believe that a man in RSPCA uniform but also in the latest-model Mercedes convertible, can be anything other than an imposter, a con merchant out to work some sort of fiddle. RSPCA? Oh aye. Pull t'other one, it's got bells on.

Having an assistant (unpaid) was a great help, but assistants need to be trained. A call came in that I thought I could use a hand with, and it would be good experience for Linda, so I arranged to meet her beside a lake in the town's main park where a swan was reported with fishing line around its leg. This happened all the time and, usually, the birds so entangled are fairly easy to catch and deal with, but this one only had the line around one leg and had no difficulty flying away whenever we got near to it in the rowing boat lent us by the park keeper.

Thinking of Percy the Porpoise, I could see we were in

for a frustrating time. I had my swan hook, which was a device rather like a shepherd's crook, and while I did the rowing, Linda wielded the hook. Back and forth we went, with the swan taking off as soon as Linda had it in range, to land again maybe twenty yards away.

Swan-catcher Linda had heard stories about these powerful birds breaking people's arms and legs, but I told her all that hissing and flapping was mostly bravado and, if and when we caught it, so long as we kept a hold on the wings we'd have no problems with broken bones. As well as hissing and flapping, we were also hearing shouts of amused encouragement from people in the park, including Carol who happened to be taking the children for a bike ride. They all thought this the funniest thing they'd seen in weeks.

Linda and I had to give up and come back the next day when, after another exhausting few hours, we eventually did manage to catch our prey. Some of the fishing line was wrapped very tightly round its leg, so tightly in fact that the skin had started to grow over it so we couldn't just pull it off. Linda said, 'Vet,' and off we went, to my friend who usually did wildlife work for nothing (though Linda would pay anyway if he did charge us).

We were more than surprised when he said the only way to save the swan was to amputate the leg. This was something I'd never come across before and I had no idea what the consequences might be, but he was insistent. I later discovered that nobody else of my acquaintance in the animal world had ever heard of such a thing either, and we would soon find out why.

The operation itself was risky, not the surgery but the anaesthetics. Little was understood in those days about anaesthetising birds and such matters were notoriously difficult to manage. We needn't have worried because it all went well and soon we had a swan with one good leg plus paddle and one much shorter stump.

I kept the swan in my garage rescue home for three weeks, feeding it on dry dog food that had maize in it, which I floated on water so the swan could skim it off. When I thought the bird was fit enough, I called Linda and we took it down to familiar territory, the lake in the park, not quite knowing what would happen. I expected it to swim in circles until it worked out what to do in a natural way. Big birds like swans and geese have their legs spaced wide apart, which is why they walk in such a comical way, as if they have two wooden sailor's peg-legs. Our swan had shown no ability whatever in improvising one-legged movement on land, but surely that would happen once it had mastered one-paddle swimming.

Linda was a bit of a star in the local paper, always being photographed with a rescued kingfisher while looking a million dollars, so my dear friend the badger photographer was delighted when Linda phoned him and told him the story.

He stayed on the shore while Linda and I put on waders and set off with our swan. Posing carefully for the camera, we placed it in the water and watched in dismay as it tipped over on its non-leg side, flapped its wings madly and did its best to start drowning. Four times we tried, and every time it did exactly the same, now with a small crowd watching. How do you drown the queen of waterfowl? Give her to the RSPCA to cut her leg off.

Temporarily beaten, Linda went back to her kitchen units and I to my garage with the swan, deeply concerned that we were going to have to do what maybe a different vet would have done anyway, which was euthanise it.

Next day we tried again, and the next. There was no swan whisperer to call on, and no incentive we could use to teach our swan to swim with one leg, or even to stay upright, but Linda would never admit defeat and neither would I. After many trips to the lake, the swan learned to lean over to its legside and stay up, which was when I saw I'd got something right. It did indeed swim in circles.

After a few days of that it taught itself how to swim where it wanted to swim, and so we could be happy that it was going to cope. Swans can stay on the water indefinitely if there's enough food, and really only need to come out to breed and that, we felt, was something we could worry about later. Our swan became a celebrity, the famous one-legged swan of Scorswick Park, and probably the most photographed swan in history.

19

MAKING A (VERY) BAD IMPRESSION

Before I joined the RSPCA, there was a scheme that paid inspectors for getting publicity – so much for a local press article, so much for the nationals, TV, radio and so on. This had stopped by the time I became an inspector but publicity remained an important part of the job, even if we weren't paid for it. Public donations made the RSPCA – and therefore my job – possible, and I took every opportunity I could. As a consequence, I became well known through, and had excellent relations with, the local papers and radio. They tried to give my stories good coverage, and often came to me when they were short, looking for a bit of animal magic to fill a space. I made sure that animal cruelty cases always featured strongly, and sometimes used a little tear-jerking to find a home for a lost pet.

In the run-up to Christmas, I made sure that there was something in all the local media about the potential disaster of buying someone, especially a child, a puppy or kitten as a present. That doesn't happen so much now but back then it was quite common, as were the frequent consequences, of an unwanted animal brought into the RSPCA, or tied to a farm gate and abandoned, or tied up in a sack and thrown in the river.

We often had the abandoned ones brought in too, so in the weeks after Christmas our animal rescue centres were packed tight with innocent little customers. In a bid to reduce this major welfare problem, I always tried to get myself on to the local BBC radio station, or sometimes Yorkshire Television, to make a plea on behalf of puppies and kittens not to be given as presents, and to try and bring home the reality of a situation that otherwise was clouded by cuddliness and fluffiness.

One of the tricks we used to pull on the TV required an abandoned litter of pups or kittens, and alas we were rarely without same. I would go on, do the interview holding one puppy or kitten, with a little sob story to go with it, and every time without exception the TV station's switchboard would be jammed by eager adopters. With any luck, we might find good homes for the whole litter this way, with each volunteer thinking that he or she had got the very pup or kit seen on TV. All in a good cause.

One Christmas, my very good friend on BBC Radio Leeds rang me to say they were planning a programme to be broadcast by all the Yorkshire stations, covering the whole region, and would I do an interview that they could slot in. Well, of course I would, and I agreed to bring a kitten and a puppy along for sound effects.

I would go to the small, unmanned studio the BBC had near by, where the practice was (and is) to get the key from a neighbour, let yourself in, pick up a phone and talk to someone at the station, who would tell you which buttons to press. My problem was finding the time to go to York to pick up a pup and a kitten because I didn't have any at that moment and, in the end, the interview date arrived without my accomplishing this task. So, I decided to wing it and hope for the best.

Tuned in and turned on, my interviewing friend said off-line that he hoped I'd brought some really noisy animals along, as that would add greatly to the impact of our story. Oh yes, I said, I've got them in a basket here, but I can't guarantee they'll perform to cue. Miaowing and purring and puppy-dog whimpering cannot necessarily be produced to order. They normally make noises only when they're hungry, or they're upset, or they're looking for mummy. Even so, my amiable radio presenter had every confidence.

We went through all the usual points – lifetime commitment, food and water, animals can't be left at home willy-nilly, training, veterinary expenses and so on – then my man said 'Right, Inspector Langdale, I know you have some kittens and puppies there with you. Can you describe them for us?'

This was not a problem. I had a long history of looking after such animals, so I just had to pick a few at random from memory, a brown and white pup with black socks, a ginger kitten, a tabby one, and these were on the way to recovery after being abandoned in a cardboard box in the woods and being found by a dog walker. I really laid it on thick, filling in as much of my remaining time as I could.

'That's great. Now, can you put one near the microphone and maybe we'll be able to hear it.'

At a loss to know what to do, I made an attempt at a kitten noise, a sort of mini-miaow that came out like somebody had run over a cat with a squeaky bicycle wheel. I remembered Percy Edwards on the radio doing every bird there is, and every animal too. Where were you, Percy, when I needed you?

'I don't think the acoustics in that studio can be up to scratch,' said my friend, his voice a touch strangulated. 'I'll send a memo to the maintenance department. Now (cough, splutter, excuse me), what about one of the puppies?'

If my attempt at feline calls had been terrible, you should have heard the canine. Not even the worst pop singer could have made a more horrible noise, and not even the blindest of the faithful could have believed it was a real animal. Going wuff wuff would have been better.

My friend had no comment for a moment, perhaps because he was choking. When he recovered his noncorpsing self, he came back briefly to me to thank me, then made an announcement, introducing the next stage of the programme.

'Crikey, Carter, what was that about?' he said. 'Don't give up the day job, will you?'

'Sorry, mate,' I said. 'Never mind. You can edit those bits out.'

'Edit them out? A trifle late for that. Carter Langdale, famous animal impressionist, has just made his debut live across the whole of Yorkshire and beyond. The engineers here have already got you on the Christmas tape.'

20

A PRIMATE THAT PREFERRED CORNFLAKES TO PORRIDGE

Every United Nations country is signed up to the Convention on International Trade in Endangered Species (CITES), which regulates or prohibits trade in all the primate species (except us) depending on how immediate their danger is. In some countries, such as Israel and the Netherlands, there are national laws prohibiting the keeping of primates as pets, and in the UK we have the Dangerous Wild Animals Act and a licensing system. There are campaigning societies, sanctuaries, charities, and public opinion. For instance, most people in the UK now disagree with keeping primates as pets, yet the number – mostly small monkeys – being kept has stayed fairly steady over the years, in the low thousands, perhaps as many as three thousand. Nobody can say how many of these are legally bred, or how many are illegally farmed, or caught wild and illegally imported.

In the wild, primates live only with others of the same species. They are social animals. Having a single monkey in a house with a few humans is as disastrous for the monkey as it would be for you, were you to find yourself naked and alone, hoping to get along with a family of gorillas. Yes, dogs are social animals too, but a dog will adopt a human, or a family of humans, as its pack-mates. A monkey will not do that.

Why do people want to keep such an unsuitable animal as a companion or, worse, as a curiosity? Good question. We can say, however, that anyone stupid enough to buy a primate as a pet will probably not do so again. Having a monkey in the house is nothing at all like having a dog or a gerbil. It is much more like having a highly agile, physically capable human baby, except that the baby will almost certainly die.

Of course, that is the way we think now. Things used to be different – very different before the Act of 1976, and even after that for years. In the 1960s and early 70s it became fashionable among various classes of society to have unusual pets and the Act was a response to that foolishness. It gave local authorities the power to license the keeping of a wild animal, to refuse licences and to seize unlicensed animals; also it defined which were the animals, from aardvarks and alligators to vipers and wandering spiders and back again, including many of the monkeys and apes.

This Act supposedly stopped you from ringing up a

dealer and buying a tiger, an emu or a giant panda but, regardless of licensing, you could still order a monkey from *Exchange & Mart* or *Cage and Aviary* magazine, which is what the chap who called me had done. Actually, it was his wife who called, who sounded on the phone rather like Carol sometimes does when she believes I have failed the common-sense test.

She told me the story. A wooden crate had been delivered that supposedly contained a marmoset. These are very small monkeys, only eight inches tall, from Brazil. They were among the least endangered of primates and, not being on the 1976 Act list, did not require a licence to be kept. In the wild, they live in family groups of a dozen or fifteen and have a specialised diet that includes tree sap, which they get by digging into trees with their claw-like nails, insects and fruit in season. Being considered a tasty morsel by many predators, they are very watchful and alert to danger but their small size and sweet, pretty appearance, made (and makes) them a monkey of choice among those crazy folk searching the classified ads.

Our man hadn't questioned why the crate was so big, something about the size of a tea chest cut in half. Obviously, this was to make monkey transport more comfortable. He'd knelt down and peered through one of the air holes drilled in the box sides. All he could see was an eye, like his own, looking at him with equal curiosity. Crawling round and looking through more holes produced the same result: an eye.

This wasn't getting him anywhere so he'd taken a hammer and chisel to the box top. The wood came away but so did the layer of wire mesh beneath, revealing not a sweet little marmoset but a much bigger animal and a fierce one at that, which leapt at our man and bit his hand to the bone. Shrieking in pain and shock, he fell over backwards, while the gorilla or whatever it was hurtled around the hallway, swinging from the light fittings, ripping curtains from the window, knocking pictures off the wall and vases off the shelf, and generally wrecking the joint, screaming in fury all the time.

The man's wife, showing more presence of mind than her husband and telling him what she thought of his choice of pet, chased their guest into the kitchen, shut the door, found the telephone luckily still attached to the outside world, and called the RSPCA, the front-line emergency service when you have an escaped wild animal in the kitchen.

When I turned up, the man was sitting in a chair looking decidedly miserable, with one hand oozing blood through a thick layer of bandages. I listened to his side of the tale, frequently interrupted by an extremely cross wife who completely failed to see that, as her husband claimed, it was all the fault of the supplier who had sent the wrong beast. From their description, it sounded like a baboon. Baboons are among the largest of the African primates, growing to four feet tall. This one they said was about three feet, so it was a young one but still it had the highly functional canine teeth of the species, of which our man had had intimate experience.

I got quite excited. I'd never been close to a baboon before. I went to the kitchen door and listened. All was quiet, so I opened the door a fraction. Couldn't see him so I opened a bit more. I could hear him all right, chuntering away somewhere behind the door, and what I could see was almost beyond belief. The floor was covered with a mountain of pots and pans, broken crockery, broken glass, and the entire contents of the cutlery drawer. Well, you know what's in your own kitchen. Imagine emptying all the cupboards and drawers and throwing the lot all over the place, and you have the picture.

Worse, this clever near-human, presumably hungry after his journey, had sampled everything edible that he could find. Things in packets were no problem, so there was cocoa, sugar, lentils, tea, gravy powder, spaghetti, everything, everywhere. He'd clearly learned how to open jars because coffee powder, marmalade and pickled onions were added to the mess, and his attempts to get ketchup, salad cream and brown sauce out of the bottles had given the walls and ceiling a whole new colour scheme.

I retreated quietly to my van and came back with my largest basket and my grasper. Pushing the basket ahead of me through the door, I sneaked into the kitchen and shut myself in. There he was, in the corner, sitting on the work surface – and what a sight. I'm afraid I had to laugh at him because he was covered from head to foot in flour and porridge oats, smeared all over with jam and whatever, while chewing the contents of the bread bin. Baboons will eat almost anything that can be eaten, and he was demonstrating this for a fact.

He couldn't see the joke at all but he saw me, and he went mad, running up and down the worktop, screaming his defiance and baring his very impressive teeth. When I picked up my grasper he went even crazier, throwing anything that came to hand. He hadn't learned how to open tins but he knew how to throw them accurately and hard. Sugar lumps didn't hurt and he ate most of them anyway, but knives, scissors and cans of beans I had to dodge, or not as I was trying to stand there calmly, waiting for the storm to abate.

After ten minutes or so, he settled down to chomp his way through a packet of cornflakes, lubricated by finger-scrapings from a jar of Marmite, and I tried to creep up on him, grasper in hand. Very slowly I reached out but as soon as the loop was anywhere near his head he knocked it away. This went on for another ten minutes and, for the moment, I conceded. I had to try a different plan.

As standard issue, we had tranquilliser tablets that were supposed to help us subdue violent animals, although instructions were never specific about how we got said animals to swallow a tablet; they were mainly used as a painkiller and calmative for animals injured in an accident. Just a few days before, I had used one on a dog that had been hit by a car and given a broken leg so, I thought, maybe they would work with a baboon. I asked the lady to pop out to the shop to get some bananas.

Back in the kitchen, the baboon hadn't moved but had turned his attention from the cornflakes to a jar of stuffed olives. Bravely I turned my back on him, so he couldn't see me peeling away some of the skin of a banana, pushing two tranquilliser tablets into the fruit, and smoothing the skin back up. I held it out. He grabbed it eagerly, whipped the skin off faster than the eye could see and munched his way through, pausing only very briefly to spit my tablets across the room.

Baboons' faces are not as expressive as some primates' but 'Where's my next banana, idiot?' was clear enough. I had no more ideas other than to keep trying, so that's what I did. Four bananas and eight spat-out tablets later, I really had nothing to say to the increasingly impatient lady on the other side of the kitchen door. Remember, at this point she hadn't seen what I'd seen, although she might have guessed some of it after witnessing the destruction of her hallway.

Realising there were no more bananas, the baboon became angry, running up and down the worktop again then leaping up to grab the central light fitting. I didn't know if he'd pull it down or use it as a staging post in his attack on me. In fact, he returned to his favourite place and cast around for something else to eat. Nothing caught his eye, so he threw a few more tins at me and went back to his cornflakes.

The only tactic I had left was to bore him into submission. It took another twenty minutes at least before he couldn't be bothered to knock the grasper away, and I got him.

I'd had some big dogs in my grasper before then, but even the most powerful Rottweiler was nothing compared to a baboon on the end of a fishing rod. I was bigger, stronger and more intelligent, I said to myself, and therefore I must eventually emerge the victor in this unique battle, RSPCA inspector versus mad baboon. I'd decided long ago that my basket was never going to be up to the job so the bleeding husband had been made ready with the original box, a hammer and nails. He came in with the box, I held the beast down in it with my grasper, he whacked some nails in and I pulled my grasper wire free.

As we shuffled out of the kitchen with our burden, the woman came in to see, for the first time, the mind-boggling mess that only a determined gang of ten primary-school children, or one baboon, could have made. Not surprisingly, she was speechless, but the looks she was giving her husband spoke volumes. He sounded rather dispirited when making his lame promise to forgo all thoughts of ever having a monkey as a pet, and wondering what were his chances of getting compensation from the dealer.

I thought those chances were about the same as those of the dealer getting him to pay the bill for laundering a flour-caked baboon. I could go home, change, and send my uniform to the cleaners. They had a house and a marriage to mend. The baboon went back to the dealer.

21

A CALL NOT MEANT
FOR ME

We inspectors in those days were the resource everyone turned to, whenever there was any kind of a problem with any kind of an animal, and we were thoroughly trained, in depth and breadth, to cope with whatever the world might throw at us, with one serious exception. There wasn't – and still isn't – any training in covert investigation, as one might want to do if confronted by animal crime, especially wildlife crime.

Among the established forces of law and order, there is a great deal of skill and training in such investigations, but animal crime, especially wildlife crime, is not a high priority. Ordinary police officers, trained as they are to deal with crimes committed by humans against other humans, will have had no experience with badger diggers, cock- and dog-fighters, rare-egg thieves, hare coursers, deer poachers, salmon poachers, horse thieves, sheep rustlers, and so on. Although every one of our police forces appoints at least one and sometimes two wildlife officers, they can never hope to combat everything that goes on in the woods, fields and rivers.

Our chief interest in the RSPCA of course was crime involving animal cruelty, suffering and illegal killing but, because we inspectors lacked investigative training – or encouragement, come to that – the tendency was always to concentrate on the stuff we knew we could handle. We would tend to ignore the things we were not confident about, or we'd pass them to the police, even when we knew that probably nothing would be done.

I'm sure I must have been guilty of this on occasions, with an equal measure of frustration that investigating crime, with all the attendant skills and abilities such as surveillance and undercover evidence gathering, was beyond an officer like me, already with too much work to do.

My life turned a corner one weekend, one of my double-duty covering weekends, when calls from a more northerly district were diverted to me. A young chap rang, who told me he and his wife had moved two or three years before into a small village up on the North Yorks moors and, over that time, had become increasingly concerned at what they saw as a decline in wildlife. They were keen birdwatchers and wildlife spotters in general, and they had realised that something was going wrong.

Central to it all, they were sure, was an elderly man, a retired gamekeeper, who had been recruited part-time by a local landowner to look after the pheasants for a small shoot. This old keeper seemed to be taking his duties very seriously indeed.

On one evening walk, out with the dog, the young couple had found a dead tawny owl hanging from a tree and, near by, a pole trap. This is a spring-loaded device like a small gin trap, called a pole trap because that's where they are put, on top of a pole, in the knowledge that such a perch will be used by a raptor, to survey the ground, to launch an attack, or as a plucking post when the raptor already has its prey. The trap springs when the bird lands, crushing its legs. As the bird struggles, the trap falls off the post and dangles on a chain, leaving the bird hanging upside down to die slowly (if it hasn't died of shock), or to be killed when the trapper turns up to inspect his grisly machine.

The use of spring-loaded traps 'in an elevated position' to catch birds has been illegal in the UK since 1904, not that any legislation will prevent certain types of gamekeeper from persecuting raptors in order to protect pheasants being reared and fattened for the shoot. Nor will it deter a certain type of landowner, who may issue a warning to a gamekeeper should he see a bird of prey flying in his piece of sky, or a fox or a stoat roaming around, which warning, if it does not have the desired result, could lead to the gamekeeper being sacked.

No landowner would admit to this, so the gamekeeper

takes all the risk of being caught, but it's all happening on private land. The keeper may feel free and safe to shoot, trap or poison any animal, and may well go through his whole career without any irritating do-gooders interfering with ancient practices.

'Do-gooders' was how my young couple were being seen in the village, after asking in the pub about this gamekeeper, Mr Bagshaw, and dead tawny owls. Classed as townies, off-comers, putting their noses into local affairs they didn't understand, they were told to mind their own business. There were no threats, as there might have been on a major country estate, when a compromised gamekeeper may not have been averse to throwing a lump of poisoned meat into a do-gooder's garden where a pet dog might get it. Even so, there was an unwelcoming, unfriendly feeling that the couple felt they would have to live down, while also feeling they must do something about this keeper.

There were public footpaths that took them near the pheasant pens, and they'd found more traps and more dead owls. By inspecting the bodies, they could see that the keeper, on finding a bird alive, would bash its head against a tree. He'd then hang it up, ostensibly as a warning to other predators although nobody believed that such a warning would have the slightest effect. It was more of a trophy display, like the keepers of old who used to hang their hunters on a line, sometimes called a gibbet line, where their employers could see how well they were doing at eliminating everything that threatened their sport, from otters to weasels, from buzzards to kestrels.

The really odd thing, the couple felt, was the over-all decline in wildlife, as if this part of the National Park had become a no-go area for everything except people and pheasants. I explained how this could have happened: that if the gamekeeper was prosecuting all the birds and animals that could harm his pheasants – kestrels, sparrowhawks, foxes, badgers, weasels, stoats, even hedgehogs – the unspoken message would go round and, while the mice and the voles would be happier, the predators would disappear.

The couple had phoned the police but nothing had happened. In earlier times you might have expected the village bobby to have had a quiet word – don't overstep the line, nod's as good as a wink – but there were no village bobbies any more and the North Yorkshire Constabulary had no resources to spare to keep tabs on a semi-retired gamekeeper. Phoning me, the couple felt they had gone as far as they could without being drummed out of the village. I guaranteed their anonymity, saying I would not need their testimony because I would gather all the evidence myself. They were much relieved. Then I sat down and realised I didn't have the slightest idea about how to go about fulfilling my promise.

No good phoning the police, obviously. No good phoning colleagues as they'd be just as bemused as I was. Although I had heard of inspectors targeting song-bird trappers, I didn't know who or where. So, I thought, in the best traditions of Miss Marple, I would take my dog for a walk around that village, through the woods, and along the footpaths, and take note of everything I saw, no matter how insignificant. I took the magnetic signs off the van and set out.

I got very little out of that first trip apart from a distinct impression that this was a rather closed community, as you often find in remote rural areas – or used to find, should I say. Hardly anywhere can be classed as remote these days. In the pub, saying nothing that could give a hint why I was there, I was an object of mild North Yorkshire curiosity, given much the same treatment as, say, a Martian or a Sioux chieftain would have had, causing no more than the smallest ripple on the pond of village life.

On the way home I decided on a plan of action. A second secret trip was required, to follow the rest of the footpaths that I'd missed and find the pheasant pens and the pole traps. I'd then make a third trip, also arriving in the early-morning darkness, hide in the bushes, and wait. Meanwhile, I'd visit the Army and Navy stores to get some camouflage clothing. There were no small video recorders then, and I didn't have a decent camera, so my spying equipment consisted of my birdwatching binoculars. I had no notion then of proper concealment techniques, or how to avoid leaving traces of my movements. I had no plan about what to do should my quarry turn up with a 12-bore, and likewise no plan about how to confront him, unarmed I hoped, or what to do if he ran for it.

From phone conversations with the young couple I was able to plot the locations of the pens on the OS map and check them out on my second visit. I wanted to see what other traps there might be, such as gins for foxes, poisoned eggs for stoats and weasels, and what precautions our man had taken against poachers. We were in late spring, so the birds would be of a nice small size for the gourmet restaurant trade, or they might be lifted wholesale and taken to another shoot.

On my next weekend off, I left home in the early hours, with a somewhat sketchy explanation to Carol of what I was doing, but I hadn't left early enough. Dawn was breaking when I got there, so I just had time to pinpoint one of the pens before broad daylight made discovery too likely.

A fortnight later, weekend off again, I left soon after midnight and had plenty of time to scout around. 'Scout' was the right word, really, as I was trying to imagine what Tonto would have done if the Lone Ranger had wanted him to find a trail. Many gamekeepers pass this way, Kemosabe, I said to myself as I prowled around with my little torch with the red filter, trying to improve my night vision by using only one eye at a time, which I'd read somewhere was what the gunners did in the bombers during the war. Anyway, I found the second pen, and a pole that had been used with a trap but which had no trap set just then, and no other traps or defensive measures.

On the one hand I'd found some evidence, real evidence. On the other, I had no way of linking it to anyone in particular, and I'd had my first experience of how frustrating such work can be, occupying many hours, always with the tensions of secrecy, and so often coming away with nothing.

Nothing would not do, so I resolved to return again. Another two weeks of normal duties went by. I cooked up another vague story for Carol to explain why I was leaving the house at midnight on a Saturday. I don't suppose she believed it but she would have known that whatever I was up to, it would be to do with my obsession with animals, to which everything else came second.

I got to the village in plenty of time, parked up, walked the two miles in to my target area, and checked out the first pen. Nothing there, so on to the second pen, where I found a trap set on the previously empty pole with nothing in it. I did a wider circuit, hoping. Then I saw it. About fifty yards away, a dim shadow in my red torchlight, there was a pole with something hanging down.

Heart bumping, I went up close. Now I could see it was an owl, not moving. And now was the moment of decision. I had to do something, I knew that, but what? I couldn't keep coming back here every other weekend until some sort of a miracle occurred. Whatever was going to be the result of this, my first secret investigation of crime, it was down to me to make it happen.

The keeper would surely come to look at his trap, but

would it be this morning? There was no option. I hid in among some brambles and waited. Soon I discovered another truth about this sort of work, in a wood, in the dark, alone, with no back-up. It's spooky, cold, eerie, unnerving and decidedly stressful if you're not used to it. Without giving it that technical name, I was doing covert surveillance, and there's another characteristic of that: you don't know how slowly time can pass until you've crouched on your own, in a bush on a cold night, waiting for the dawn.

I still didn't really know what I would do if my man appeared, with or without a shotgun, with or without a large, violent companion. All senses were on full alert, while the body was sending messages about the chill and the cramps brought about by staying in the same position for a long time. I hadn't thought about wearing thermals under my cotton camouflage gear, nor of bringing a flask of hot coffee, nor had I realised that breathing out into the still, cold air, just as the sun was touching the horizon, made a cloud of steam that anyone could see. I'd have been less discoverable waving a flag. I had no mask or scarf to put over my mouth, so all I could do was use my hand as a deflector.

Three hours later I was about to give up. The sun was shining, the birds were singing, I was aching all over, and someone was heading my way. A small hunched figure of a man appeared, scruffily dressed in an old wax jacket and a trilby hat, walking with a hefty stick. If this was an eccentric millionaire, he was making a very good job of looking more or less destitute. Mr Bagshaw it had to be.

He went up to the pole trap, fumbled inside his jacket and took out a hessian sack that he put on the ground. I thought, I'm watching this, and he's not even bothering to look around, but why would he? He had no need to worry. He was in the middle of the woods, on private land and, as far as he was concerned, on private business, a long way from the nearest nosy parker.

As he disconnected the trap from the pole, the owl, dangling down, flapped its wings. God Almighty, it was still alive! With racing mind and no strategy at all, I jumped out of the undergrowth and shouted 'RSPCA!'

A smarter chap than this one would have said 'Oh, jolly good, glad to see you. Just on a walk through the woods and, do you know, came across this trap. Poor thing. They're illegal, aren't they?'

Instead, he stood there, almost fainting with shock and surprise, his jaw dropped as far as it would go. I walked up to him, brandishing my ID card like someone from a TV cop programme, sprung the owl from its trap and stuffed it inside my jacket. I didn't have a lot of hope for it but I always had to try. I checked inside the sack: dead tawny owl.

I'd learned from my dealings with other kinds of animal abusers that you must always take the high ground and stick to it. Authority, dominance, self-assurance – all these must be apparent from your behaviour and demeanour, so I wasted no time with this fellow. However, I couldn't quite manage the full formality of speech that I would have liked.

'Mr Bagshaw, I am arresting you on suspicion of causing the death of a protected species, and of using traps that you're not allowed to. You are not obliged to say anything, but if you do say anything, I'll write it down. Now, we'll go back to yours.'

He led the way. His ruddy complexion had paled to grey and he walked like a condemned man to the scaffold. I had the sack, with the trap and the dead owl, so the evidence was there in plenty. The owl inside my jacket wasn't moving and I was anxious to start doing something for it. I would keep the interview to a minimum and come back again later.

His little cottage on the edge of the woods was typical. Unobtrusive, badly maintained on the outside, and full of gamekeepers' treasures within – fox masks on the wall, all sorts of trophies and old pictures, a stuffed badger, fox-skin hearthrug, more old pictures including some rather nice early hunting prints, a bunch of fox brushes, a stuffed sparrowhawk.

We sat at the kitchen table. I told him that I knew he had been killing tawny owls with pole traps and he admitted it. He was a gamekeeper, charged with looking after pheasant poults, and he'd had trouble with owls taking them. The boss had told him he'd better not lose many more or he'd be singing for his wages – and his job next year. He knew it was illegal, but what was he suppose to do?

I told him I'd be back to take a full statement, and headed off to my van in a state of mild euphoria. The irony did not escape me that the excitement and satisfaction I was feeling was all to do with the thrill of the hunt, the exhilaration of the chase and the kill, only the animal I had been hunting knew why, and had earned his punishment.

My owl seemed beyond help but I put it in a small basket in the passenger footwell of the van and turned the heater on full. I was hardly halfway home before it was showing me how wrong I'd been, and so my first stop became the vet's. This owl has a broken leg and concussion, he said, but you can collect it in the morning.

After several cups of tea and a fried egg sandwich, and a brief explanation to Carol, I rang the young couple. They were overjoyed, as I was. Only Carol seemed less than enthusiastic.

'What's the matter?' I said.

'You've got the bug,' she replied. 'I can see it. Being an ordinary RSPCA inspector isn't going to be enough any more. James bloody Bond more like.'

Carol had a point but it would be a while before her prophesy came true.

I went back to see Bagshaw. He admitted everything and signed my notebook to that effect. I had a trap, and a dead tawny owl with broken leg and fractured skull.

All the papers went off to headquarters and I waited

eagerly for the court case to be set up but it wasn't going to happen. Because Bagshaw was seventy-four years old, it was decided that it was not in the public interest to put him through court. Instead he was issued with a formal warning. I tried to persuade HQ otherwise but failed. Still, it had been a good job if you stood back and looked.

The young couple kept me informed about the woods around their village. The shoot had been closed down. Mr Bagshaw was seen only at the shop and the pub. And the wildlife was flourishing again. All the birds and mammals were back as if peace had been declared. My tawny owl was shown to be blind in one eye and, although its leg was set and mended, it couldn't go back to the wild. I gave it to a local enthusiast I knew well, and he kept it in his aviary where it lived a long and relatively happy life.

As for me, well, Carol was right of course. I had got the bug. Over the next few years I mounted quite a few covert investigations, learning something new from every one. Eventually I became the first full-time undercover investigator of animal crime in the world – but that's another story altogether.